BLOODY BRITISH HISTORY
HISTORY

OXFORD

PAUL SULLIVAN

The History

3302696451

For Jay, Jan and Theo.

Thanks to:

*My parents Marlene and Terry Sullivan, who once again provided
the space, food and tea that enabled me to finish the book.*

*Magda Bezdekova, who provided fruit and veg, transport
and countless back issues of* Oxford Today.

*Oxford residents and great pals Geoff Morgan and Sarah Day
for their generosity of spirit, praise and hospitality.*

*Cate Ludlow at The History Press for being so Bloody minded, and Declan Flynn for
proof reading.*

The History Press
The Mill, Brimscombe Port
Stroud, Gloucestershire, GL5 2QG
www.thehistorypress.co.uk

© Paul Sullivan, 2012

The right of Paul Sullivan to be identified as the Author
of this work has been asserted in accordance with the
Copyrights, Designs and Patents Act 1988.

All rights reserved. No part of this book may be reprinted
or reproduced or utilised in any form or by any electronic,
mechanical or other means, now known or hereafter invented,
including photocopying and recording, or in any information
storage or retrieval system, without the permission in writing
from the Publishers.
British Library Cataloguing in Publication Data.
A catalogue record for this book is available from the British Library.

ISBN 978 0 7524 6549 4

Typesetting and origination by The History Press
Printed in Great Britain

OXFORDSHIRE LIBRARY SERVICE	
3302696451	
Askews & Holts	22-Oct-2012
942.574	£9.99

CONTENTS

THE DARKEST OF DARK AGES

AD 912 – 'This year died Æthered ealdorman of the Mercians, and King Edward took possession of London and Oxford and of all the lands which owed obedience thereto.'

This is the earliest appearance of the name 'Oxford', although the very fact that it was worth mentioning/capturing reveals that it was an established town well before this incident.

There seems little doubt that the city was around in the ninth century, during the reign of King Alfred (founding father of the University, according to apocrypha, although hard facts have remained frustratingly elusive). The closest we come to 'evidence' is the existence of Alfred-era coins bearing the name Orsnaford, which is tantalisingly close to the Saxon Oxnaford, but not close enough to convince most modern historians. Alfred's founding of University College is an interesting tale, but there is simply no historical evidence to back it up.

So it is that the early years of Oxford – doubtless coloured by the bloody turmoil of the Saxon-versus-Dane warfare that tore the land apart several times from the eighth to the tenth centuries – are a kind of Dark-Age theme park: no written records, and just a handful of suitably vague legends.

At a crossing point on a major river, the boundary between the two mighty kingdoms of Wessex and Mercia, it stands to reason that there should have been an important settlement. The very fact that King Edward 'the Elder' (son of Alfred) took control of the town after the death of Æthered indicates that Oxford was of strategic importance. That year 912 marks the fortification of the city and the building of its walls – a true origin, of sorts.

Legend, undeterred by the absence of hard fact, takes Oxford much further into the past. According to the stories that used

King Alfred.

Julius Caesar: relics from his era may still be found in Oxford.

to pass for history before people started taking the subject seriously, when Alfred revivified the city in the ninth century he was building on truly ancient foundations. Under the British language name Caer Memphric, and later Rydychen or Bos Vadum (in Latin), both meaning 'oxen ford', the settlement was founded in 1009 BC by King Memphric (aka Mempricius). This was according to the wild imagination of Geoffrey of Monmouth, an early Oxford scholar most famous for his invention of various fundamental bits of the King Arthur legends. His invented Memphric wasn't a very good patron to have: he raped and pillaged his own country, causing it to melt down in civil war. He was eventually eaten by wolves during a hunting trip near Caer Memphric.

This foundation was confirmed by later historians, right through to William Stukeley in the eighteenth century, and half-heartedly allowed to pass through the gates of reason by some early nineteenth-century writers. Nathanial Whittock, writing in 1828, acknowledges John Ross (most famous for his 1607 book *Britannica*, which was no more than a poetical rendering of Geoffrey of Monmouth's work) for 'penetrating the thick clouds of ages past, and proving the founding of Oxford to have taken place before the erection of Solomon's Temple ... it is quite certain that a town was built on this spot in the time of the aboriginal Britons'. The castle was said to be the site of the original city.

In spite of these ancient mythical beginnings, the city played little part in the legends that plug the gap between 1009 BC and recorded history. According to Geoffrey, King Arthur was on the verge of conquering Rome in the fifth century when another outbreak of civil war back home brought him to his muddy death in the Battle of Camlann. This led to decades of weak leadership and rudderless squabbling, opening the gates to the Anglo-Saxon invaders whose descendant Alfred eventually rebuilt the faded glories of Oxford.

Disreputable origins, glorious heydays, decline and fall, death and rebirth – it's no wonder this version of Oxford's history has had such appeal over the years.

WHAT DID THE ROMANS DO FOR US?

The oddest thing about Oxford history is its lack of Romans. But, once again, this did not trouble the pseudo-historians, who invented a spot of Armageddon to set the scene for Alfred's renaissance. According to Whittock, 'in the year 50 this town suffered its most terrible downfall, being reduced to ashes by the Roman general Plautus, in the reign of Julius Caesar, and only retained its original name from its still continuing a Ford for Oxen.'

KING ALFRED IN OXFORD

King Alfred the Great was born in Wantage and, whether he founded the city of Oxford or not (endowing the University in 872, according to legend), he was certainly familiar with the area. He spent much of his reign at war with the Danish Vikings, a campaign culminating in the Battle of Ashdown on 8 January 871, close to Oxford in a part of the county which, before 1974, was in Berkshire.

The Danes, under King Bagsecg, fresh from victory against the Saxons at Reading, marched to Ashdown to meet Wessex King Ethelred and his brother Alfred's armies. The Danes had the advantage of arms and tactics, but the Saxons had potentially more men – as long as they could summon them in the first place.

According to the legend, the young prince rode to Blowingstone Hill at Kingston Lisle and put his lips to the Blowing Stone. Only a skilled player could get a note out of this unpromising sarsen stone instrument, and only a man born to be King could make that note heard across the surrounding downs as far as White Horse Hill (a legend that still holds, if anyone fancies having a go).

He hit the right note, and the army came racing to his side. The Battle of Ashdown was a victory for Alfred, and King Bacsecg and his chief earls were slain. Alfred became King in March 871, after Ethelred was killed in battle. But the wars only ceased when Alfred beat Danish King Guthrum to a standstill at the Battle of Ethandun in Wiltshire, 878, paving the way for the treaty of partition that created the Danelaw in the north of the island.

This appears to be a garbled reference to the attempts of Aulus Plautus to conquer Britain during the reign of Emperor Claudius in AD 43. Plautus occupied the south of the island and received the surrender of eleven British Kings, bringing Britain under the Roman yoke over the next four years, but there is no mention in the records of Bos Vadum.

It is more historically accurate to state that the Romans had small settlements in the immediate vicinity, north and east of the present city centre. A dog's bones were discovered in the foundations of a first-century AD wall at the site of the Churchill kilns, on the site of the Churchill Hospital. The remains were found alongside human bones – both had been placed at the foundations as sacrificial offerings. The Romano-British residents believed that the spirit of the dog would protect the wall from being overthrown. The spirit of the man was probably there to throw a few sticks during history's quieter periods.

The same Churchill site, in addition to this earliest known Oxford dog, also yielded the earliest named human in these parts: Tamesibugus. A fragment of pottery found here, and now on display in the Museum of Oxford, bears the legend 'TAMESIBUGUS FECIT', translating as 'Thames-dweller made it'.

THE EMERGENCE OF OXFORD

After the withdrawal of the Romans and the invasion of the proto-English, the old area of pre-Saxon settlements, based around modern Headington, seems to have been encompassed by a royal estate.

Beaumont Palace.

A mere 8 miles south, St Birinus was installed as Bishop of Dorchester in the 630s, the small town being one of the most important Christian HQs in the island. St Frideswide was a living legend in these parts later in the century, and local history was in full swing. All it lacked was that all-important 'Oxford' tag.

The first death in Oxford is recorded in the *Anglo-Saxon Chronicle* for the year AD 924: 'This year King Edward died among the Mercians at Farndon; and very shortly, about sixteen days after this, Elward his son died at Oxford; and their bodies lie at Winchester.'

This was the beginning of a long association between Oxford and royalty, based for many centuries on the twelfth century royal palace at Beaumont (source of the name of modern Beaumont Street). Its site is marked with a plaque recording the birth here of Richard the Lionheart and King John; by which time Oxford had been baptised in blood several times over.

THE CURSE OF SAINT FRIDESWIDE

PRINCESS FRIDESWIDE (MORE properly, but less pronounceably, Fritheswithe) was born in around 665 AD, the daughter of King Didan and Queen Sefrida, who ruled a region equivalent to modern-day Berkshire and a big chunk of south-west Oxfordshire. The royal family were Christians, in an era when many of the neighbours were still invoking Germanic pagan deities Woden, Thunor and Freya rather than Father, Son and Holy Ghost. So keen were Didan and Sefrida on the newly imported religion that they put Frideswide under the tutelage of local holy woman Ælfgith, where she became enlightened both academically and spiritually. It was a case of brains and beauty, as Frideswide was said to be in the Helen of Troy league when it came to good looks.

After Ælfgith's death Frideswide returned to the palace, and for an unorthodox birthday present asked her father to build a church on the edge of Oxford (a few centuries before the city appears in any historical document). He complied, and Frideswide took twelve likeminded girls and fitted the place out as a convent. The proto-nuns didn't opt for the cloistered life; but remaining visible to the wicked world was nearly Frideswide's downfall.

Pagan lust is not an emotion to be trifled with. When Algar, the heathen King of neighbouring Mercia, heard of the royal nun's beauty he took his pagan posse over the border to seek her hand, and all the other bits, in marriage. King Didan didn't do much to stop him, Algar being lord of a sizeable kingdom, and a definite 'catch'. But Frideswide announced that her holy vow of chastity removed her permanently from the matrimonial market. In response,

Anglo-Saxon King, from a contemporary engraving.

Frideswide hiding from Algar: a stained-glass window in Christ Church, Oxford.

Algar announced that if she would not marry him willingly he would throw her over the back of his horse, carry her to said market and marry her at sword-point.

Recognising a violent sexual metaphor when she saw one, Frideswide decided it was time to flee. Algar's men made a rush to capture her, but were struck blind by divine intervention. The princess then put on her running shoes, and reaching the Thames she hijacked a boat and disappeared into the night. The place is most commonly given as Frilsham in Berkshire, but some say she ended up at Bampton in Oxfordshire; others cite the location as Binsey (now part of Oxford).

Here Frideswide hid in a pig shed in the middle of an oak wood. The swineherd allowed her to look after his animals, a novel way for a holy woman to bring home the bacon, and she made the best of a bad job by praying to God for a clean water supply. A well obligingly sprang up, and she fed and watered herself here for three years.

When this time had elapsed, Frideswide thought it safe to tiptoe back to the nunnery. But her twelve acolytes had hardly had time to uncork a celebratory bottle of communion wine before Algar stormed back to the city, his spies having revealed that the beautiful princess had returned. King Didan risked everything by sending an army to thwart the merciless Mercian, but Algar's host was too strong. The battered Berkshire men retreated, and the Mercians prepared to burn Oxford to the ground. Furthermore, Algar announced, he would not only ravish the unfortunate Frideswide in revenge for her disobedience, but would allow his men to have their extremely wicked ways with her too. Torches were lit, the pre-Oxford Oxford cursed itself for being made of wood and thatch, and all hope fled. But Frideswide

HENRY THE FATE

Frideswide's curse kept troublesome royalty away for the best part of 900 years. The first monarch to dismiss the legend was Henry VIII, who allowed St Frideswide's Priory to be dissolved and converted into a University College by Cardinal Wolsey. Some people put Henry's subsequent problems and deathbed agonies (he died with the words 'All is lost! Monks, monks, monks!', according to legend), down to his cavalier approach to this curse.

directed some well-chosen prayers at Saints Catherine and Cecilia – both of whom had chosen death over ravishment – and they swiftly intervened. There was a flash of lightning, and this time it was Algar who was struck blind.

Dismayed at this second show of divine long-sightedness, the Mercians called a halt to their attack. Frideswide made Algar swear that he would pursue her no longer; and receiving his promise she returned to her holy life, giving warning that henceforth any King who attempted to enter the city with violent intent would suffer the same fate as Algar. For complying with these terms, Algar was given back his sight.

Frideswide lived out her remaining years in peace, her fame and holiness acting as a magnet for donations to the priory, which soon became rich. It also became a bit big and bustling for Frideswide, who ended her days in a smaller nunnery at Binsey, where she caused a second magical holy well to spring forth - the still-flowing Treacle Well. The sticky name simply means 'medicinal', 'treacle' being a word for a healing balm. Pilgrims with all manner of ailments would visit the spot to seek a cure. Local wag Lewis Carroll found the name irresistible, using it as the basis for the genuinely sticky Treacle Well in Alice in Wonderland.

She died there in AD 735, becoming a saint some 400 years later.

St Margaret's Well. (Steve Roberts)

RELICS OF ST FRIDESWIDE

- Christ Church Cathedral is believed to stand on the foundations of Frideswide's original church. Seventh-century graves on the site corroborate the theory.
- The original church was burnt down during a massacre of Oxford's Danish residents in 1002, but in 1122 St Frideswide's Priory was erected on the same spot.
- In 1180 the prior disinterred some bones alleged to be Frideswide's and placed them in a reliquary at her shrine inside the church. Pilgrims loved it, and the church in turn loved all the money they dropped in the donation boxes. That, after all, is what relics were all about.
- A new shrine was built in 1289, but was smashed to bits by the bully boys of the Protestant Reformation in the 1530s. The bits have since been glued back together, and the results can be seen in Christ Church's Latin Chapel, coloured by a Frideswide-themed 1850s stained glass window by Pre-Raphaelite artist Edward Burne-Jones.
- Oxford Cathedral is the former St Frideswide's priory church, surviving intact as part of Cardinal Wolsey's Cardinal College. This short-lived institution was renamed King Henry VIII's College when it was commandeered by Henry in 1532, and refounded as Christ Church in 1546, at which point the cathedral had been partially demolished.
- Frideswide's restless bones, scattered by the Reformation, were relocated by Catholic Mary Tudor a few decades later and placed in two silk bags.
- Under Mary's successor Elizabeth, relics were outlawed. Frideswide's bits and bobs were mingled with the bones of another woman. In some versions of the story this other woman was Catherine Cathie, a runaway nun who had married an ex-friar. She was buried in the vicinity of the modern-day shrine. In another version of this tale the second set of bones belong to the wife of Peter Martyr, Protestant canon of Christ Church: they had been thrown on a dunghill in Mary's reign, before being rescued again by Elizabeth.

Christ Church (from Carfax tower), site of Frideswide's priory.

THE VIKINGS ARE COMING!

DURING THE TENTH and early eleventh centuries the south of England was raped, pillaged and plundered by Vikings in a pitiless and relentless onslaught that would be hard to exaggerate. Conjure every Viking cliché you can think of – apart from the horned helmets, which they never wore – and you'll be close to the truth.

By this time, Kings had been following the same course of action for a century. As soon as the Danes landed they waited a bit to see how violent they were going to be and how far they were going to invade from their established base on the Isle of Wight, and then bribed them into temporary submission with money ('Danegeld') and food. This usually cost them a major chunk of the local harvest, and an amount of money on a scale reminiscent of a city banker's ill-gotten bonus.

Each time this occurred, the Danish generals promised to make peace, only to repeat the whole thing a few years later. By 1002, the chronicle writers of the time had run out of words to describe the horrors of a cocky, lusty army advancing like priapic locusts through the countryside of southern England with nothing to fear except indigestion and venereal disease.

In 1002 Ethelred II was King. He was nicknamed Ethelred the Unready (his name and title together translating as 'royal counsel uncounselled'). His counsel, or lack of it, was to pay the Danes a purse-boggling sum of £24,000 (that's the city banker's salary, bonus and pension combined). But the man Ethelred sent to present the enemy with this colossal back-hander was Ealdorman Leofsy, of Danish parentage, and about as loyal as a pet cat with a grudge. Soon afterwards, Leofsy killed Ethelred's High Steward Eafy and was banished from court, amidst rumours that the Danes planned to keep the money, kill Ethelred and steal his kingdom. The luckless King suffered a classic case of 'I want my money back!'

COCKLES AND MUSCLES

The north of England was still a Danish stronghold at this point in history, and many cities in the south, including Oxford,

Coin of Ethelred II – the Vikings were bribed with coins like these.

Massacre of the Danes on St Brice's Day.

had large Danish communities too. Some of them were second generation, and were a far easier target than their sword and axe-wielding cousins in the Isle of Wight fleet. Ethelred prepared a statement and had it sent to various towns and cities,

ordering reprisals against the Danes in a concerted English act of violence on St Brice's Day, 13 November 1002. This was the traditional time for slaughtering livestock and bull baiting, and Ethelred hoped to catch the mood of bloody necessity.

In Oxford the call to arms was taken up enthusiastically, and the local Danes, vastly outnumbered, fled to the sanctuary of St Frideswide's church on the site of modern Christ Church Cathedral. They were scapegoats, victims of ethnic cleansing; but given the recent record of their ever-invading kinsmen, Viking apologists were very thin on the ground.

In 1004 Ethelred described the ensuing events matter-of-factly in a royal Charter which was drawn up to argue the case for rebuilding the destroyed church of St Frideswide's:

...to the effect that all the Danes who sprang up in this island, sprouting like cockle [a type of flower] amongst the wheat, were to be destroyed by a most just extermination, and thus this decree was to be put into effect even as far as death, those Danes who dwelt in [Oxford],

VIKINGS IN THE CELLA

Wallingford historian John de Cella (c. 1152-1214) blamed the anti-Danish mood in Oxford not on a century of bloody invasions, but on personal hygiene. The Vikings were not the smelly ones, however: 'The Danes, thanks to their habit of combing their hair every day, of bathing every Saturday and regularly changing their clothes, were able to undermine the virtue of married women and even seduce the daughters of nobles to be their mistresses.'

John de Cella, or John of Wallingford, was born as John Hyde, son of the Lord of the Manor of Denchworth in Berkshire. He was prior of Holy Trinity Priory in Wallingford and later abbot of St Albans, but is far more renowned as a historian, poet and physicist. The Oxford Massacre was captured in *Chronica Joannis Wallingford*, a historical chronicle covering the period 449 to 1036.

striving to escape death, entered this sanctuary of Christ, having broken by force the doors and bolts, and resolved to make refuge and defence for themselves therein against the people of the town and the suburbs; but when all the people in pursuit strove, forced by necessity, to drive them out, and could not, they set fire to the planks and burnt, as it seems, this church with its ornaments and its books. Afterwards, by God's aid, it was renewed by me.

The 'just extermination' did indeed involve burning down the church, its Viking contents and its fixtures and fittings (hence the need for a *Grand Designs*-like royal Charter). A few of the Danes tried to break out and flee, but they were killed on the spot. The arson was excused on the grounds that the people left inside had refused to come out and face the armed, murderous mob, a decision not altogether unfathomable.

The massacre inspired old adversary King Sweyn Forkbeard of Denmark, Norway and Sweden, to invade and add 'England' to his list a few years later. His sister Gunnhild, who was one of the hostages handed to Ethelred to seal the temporary peace before the massacre, had been killed, and he wanted revenge. A famine in 1005 delayed the Viking reprisals (a famine probably caused by the Danes' unsupportable demands on the English farmers), but in 1013 they made their move. Sweyn invaded, and conquered.

King Sweyn is written out of many history books, in spite of reigning until his death in 1014, when his son Cnut took over. The future wasn't looking very English at that point, until Cnut pulled off a crowd-pleasing political coup, marrying Emma, princess of the English (Wessex branch) royal family, giving Anglophiles a straw to clutch at.

SOMETHING FISHY IN ST GILES

The St Brice's Day Massacre was the stuff of largely unsubstantiated legend until 2010, when a mass grave at St John's College on St Giles was unearthed, a ditch containing the bones of thirty-odd violently terminated early eleventh-century Vikings.

St Giles isn't very close to Christ Church, but the ditch was probably a purpose-dug mass grave to which corpses were dragged from various bits of the city. The skeletons had an assortment of cracked skulls, wounds in spines and pelvic bones, and burns. There was also one decapitee.

The clincher came when analysis showed the bones had belonged to men who ate more fish and shellfish than the average Saxon, pointing to seafood-loving Scandinavians.

Gateway to St John's College, under which lie the bones of murdered Danes.

OXFORD IN RUINS

FROM THE MOMENT William the Conqueror first set foot in Westminster Abbey for his coronation in 1066, to the post-mortem moment when his putrefying body exploded in that same edifice twenty-two years later, the portents were bad. The streets outside the abbey during the crowning were thick with Norman soldiers, expecting Saxon insurrection at any moment. Inside the abbey, the press-ganged congregation was asked, first by the Bishop of Coutances in French, and then by the Bishop of York in English, if it supported the right of Guillaume le Bâtard, Duke of Normandy, to reign in England as King William I. Both sides shouted in the affirmative. Very loudly.

So loudly, in fact, that the twitchy troops outside thought the expected rebellion had broken out. They immediately ran to the abbey with drawn swords, some of them stopping on the way to torch the surrounding houses of the treacherous English. The combination of smoke, noise, and armed Normans sent the Saxon contingent into a panic: they fled the abbey, leaving Guillaume – visibly shaking – to receive the crown in front of a drastically reduced number of witnesses. In doing so, he used the traditional Saxon coronation oath, and promised to rule his foreign subjects as well as any English King before.

Le Bâtard clearly had a very low opinion of his predecessors on the throne, as his rule was a combination of terror, destruction and extortion. Like any other occupying force throughout history, his plan was simple: to control the people by occupying key power bases with his militia,

William the Conqueror.

taking out the lynchpins of the opposition and seizing and controlling all channels of finance and production.

One of the key power bases in the south was Oxford, and the Normans played power politics very skilfully. Unable to storm and occupy every city at once, they dazzled key Saxon Earls with dreams of dominion and promises of personal wealth. The big boss in Oxford since the brief reign of Harold II (aka Harold Godwinson, famously skewered by a Norman arrow at the Battle of Hastings) was Edgar Atheling (meaning 'the young royal'). Edgar was an important symbol for Guillaume, as he had been proclaimed King by the Saxon Witangemot, or royal council, after the death of Harold in 1066.

Edgar was the grandson of King Edmund II ('Edmund Ironside'), descended from King Alfred the Great, and he was one of the first waves of Anglo-nobility to take his place in the new Norman court.

Reinstalled as governor of Oxford, Edgar was part of the Conqueror's battle plan. With the threat of rebellion never far away, the new King acted swiftly, consolidating his position in the south by sending his army westwards, before turning his attentions to the more troublesome Midlands and North. Having the supposedly loyal Edgar on the border between the goodlands and the badlands was essential. Quite how much of a city Oxford was at this point is debatable, though: it had been stormed soon after the Hastings victory, and between 1066 and 1086 it lost more than 50 per cent of its houses, much of its area being described as 'waste'. This suggests destruction on a scale to equal anything seen in the northern cities stormed by the Normans in the years that followed the Conquest; but its exact cause – deliberate trashing, redevelopment, evacuation or disaster – remains frustratingly elusive in the tight-lipped pages of local history.

OXFORD BLUES: EDGAR'S RISE AND FALL

By the middle of 1067 the 'secured' part of the island didn't extend much further north than Oxford, with London, the south east, East Anglia, and the southern counties as far as Dorset safely in the bag. But so confident was Guillaume in his position that he sailed back to Normandy, taking with him much booty and a boatload of loyal Englishmen, including Edgar Atheling. England was left in the hands of the King's brother, Bishop Odo of Bayeaux, who commenced the ruthless repressions that would mark the next few years.

Having shown his riches to his feudal master the King of France, Guillaume returned in 1068 to consolidate his conquest at last. Oxford was militarily occupied, whether Edgar Atheling liked it or not. From this key base on their southern borders, the Normans swept into the Midlands and beyond in what was later referred to as 'the Harrying of the North'. This was largely in response to open rebellion by Harold Godwinson's brother-in-law Edwin, the Earl of Mercia, and his brother Morcar of Northumbria. But Guillaume was swift in his attack. During his army's northward march everything in its path was burnt, every stray English person was killed, and the land was poisoned. Classic 'scorched earth' policy, and brutally effective. Coupled with crippling taxes and followed up by the Domesday survey, to ensure that not a single penny, hovel or chicken went unrecorded, Guillaume finally emerged as complete Conqueror and utter Bâtard.

In Oxford and elsewhere, the secured territory was parcelled out to Norman generals and churchmen, and everything was heavily fortified. The city's first Norman overlord was Robert D'Oilly, and the Saxons who had assisted the

Conqueror's ascent to the throne now rued the day. When the Harrying reached York, Guillaume settled himself in that city, confiscating a cartload of provisions that was heading for the palace of Archbishop Aldred, the man who had crowned him in Westminster Abbey. This was too much for the hungry prelate – you would have hoped the murder, pillage and arson would have provoked him before now – who barged into Guillaume's makeshift court, allegedly declaring, 'I consecrated thee, I blessed thee, and crowned thee with mine own hand; but now I curse thee – thee and thy race, because thou hast made thyself the persecutor of God's church and the oppressor of its ministers!'

But the King let him leave in peace, doubtless confident that a spot of supper would soon take the edge off his temper.

FORTRESS OXFORD

At this point, and very late in the day, it became obvious to Edgar Atheling that his reign as an English landowner was coming to an end. Taking his mother Agatha and his sisters Margaret and Cristina, he fled to the coast and took a ship to Scotland, where he was received with honour by King Malcolm III. Malcolm had, as a young man, found refuge in the English court during the reign of a certain King Macbeth, and was happy to reciprocate. Furthermore, he later married Edgar's sister Margaret.

The descendants of these, and other, English earls in the court of King Malcolm set the seeds for several lines of the Scottish aristocracy. Edgar never quite gave up hope of seeing Oxford again, and of staking a Saxon claim for the throne of England. But Guillaume had seduced former rebels such as Morcar of Mercia and Edwin of Northumbria to swear loyalty to the Norman throne, allowing them to live as rich puppets on their former estates. Without these leading players, Edgar Atheling's hopes of claiming the crown bestowed by the Witangemot of 1066 were finally dashed.

Morcar and Edwin did not enjoy their blood money for long. Guillaume feared that their popularity would one day lead to revolution, so he launched lightning raids on their estates. However, the Saxon nobles got wind of the attacks and managed to escape. Edwin headed to

The site of Oxford Castle from an old print, showing St George's and Shire Hall.

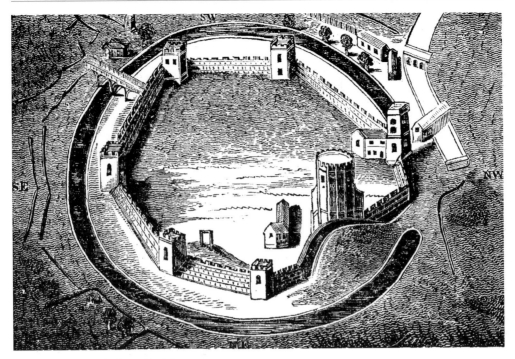

Ancient plan of Oxford Castle's defences.

Scotland but was betrayed, beheaded and delivered (without his body) to Guillaume as a gory gift. Morcar joined the soggy rebellion of Hereward the Wake in the Cambridgeshire Fenlands, where many dispossessed Saxons hoped to rise from the ashes, just as the all-but-defeated King Alfred the Great had done 200 years earlier when contemplating cakes and Vikings from his damp stronghold in Somerset.

But Alfred's comeback was indeed a one-off. Hereward's rebellion, and all the others, fizzled out. Back in Oxford, Robert D'Oilly, first High Sheriff of Oxfordshire, cleared the Saxon slums in the east of the city, built himself a castle there in 1071, along with the still-standing attendant church of St George, and applied his courtly Norman-French ways to obliterate the last traces of Edgar Atheling and the English Kings of old.

ALL WAR AND NO PEACE

KING STEPHEN WAS the nephew of King Henry I (1100-1135). Henry's only legitimate son, William Adelin, had died in a shipwreck in 1120, along with one of Henry's several illegitimate children, Richard, leaving the King's legitimate daughter, Matilda, as the direct heir. Stephen, however, disputed her claim and seized the throne, leading to a period of civil war and spectacular, lawless brutality known ever afterwards as the Anarchy.

Poor Oxford, just establishing itself as a great European seat of learning, found itself achieving unwanted fame as the city at the heart of an inter-dynastic dispute, being the chosen base of Matilda. Henry I had explicitly named her as his successor, but for various reasons she was not a popular choice. First of all, obviously, she was a woman, which did not go down well with the patriarchal Norman aristocracy. She was also wife of Geoffrey of Anjou – hence their dynasty's collective name, 'Angevins' – and Anjou was a mortal enemy of the Duchy of Normandy, having recently tried to conquer it (the Kings of England also being titled Dukes of Normandy, subservient to the King of France and at loggerheads with their various rivals in the French homelands). Matilda had spent hardly any time in England prior to Henry's death, and that did not enamour her to the Anglo-Norman mob either.

King Stephen.

Queen Matilda.

When the King died in 1135, Theobald de Blois prepared to seize the English crown; but brother Etienne (Stephen) beat him to it, having won the support of the London townsfolk. He also had a handily placed sympathetic younger brother Henri, Bishop of Winchester, to help him seize control of the Treasury and buy the support of influential religious and political ringleaders, including the Archbishop of Canterbury and Pope Innocent II. Stephen was crowned King, and was briefly triumphant.

ANGRY ANGEVINS

Luckily for Matilda, Stephen was a hopeless leader. He failed to pacify and bribe several key nobles, and alienated many more, including his brother. All these potential enemies had an alternative camp to defect to – Matilda's. With the fudge and chaos making all outcomes possible, Matilda finally had the courage to sail to England in 1139 and stake her claim to the island.

After various adventures, the heir of Henry I marched to London in triumph and was crowned Queen Matilda; but the townsfolk rose up against her, and she retreated, crown and all, to Oxford, holing up at the heavily fortified castle.

Stephen wasted no time in besieging Oxford, intending to show no further mercy to his Angevin cousin. The city was burnt, the castle was battered, and all looked lost. But, in an escape bid similar to and every bit as daring as that of the imprisoned Mr Toad in Oxonian Kenneth Graham's *Wind in the Willows*, Matilda donned a disguise and somehow slipped out of the castle one freezing winter's night. Wearing white to blend in with the snowy landscape, she crossed the frozen Thames and escaped to the stronghold of Wallingford Castle.

Oxford Castle's Norman section: Empress Matilda stayed at the castle until she was forced to make a daring escape.

Forces regrouped, and with her son Henry 'Curtmantle' (named after the short robes which he brought to the Anjou fashion scene) at her side, Matilda controlled the south west of England, while Stephen commanded much of the south east. But there were no more decisive battles, and the true horrors of the Anarchy now descended – a period possibly matched, but not exceeded by, the very grimmest events in this island's history.

WHAT'S IN A NAME?

- ⚉ King Stephen's real name, Etienne de Blois, has been largely forgotten, most British historians having favoured a more 'English' version of English history.
- ⚉ 'Plantagenet' comes from *Planta genista*, the Latin name for the Common Broom, a prickly plant whose yellow flowers Geoffrey of Anjou is said to have worn in his hat. It was first coined in the fifteenth century.
- ⚉ 'Angevin Empire' is a term for the real-estate portfolio founded by Geoffrey and enlarged by Matilda and Henry, but was first coined in 1887.
- ⚉ 'Lady of the English' – this was a contemporary term for Matilda (aka Maude), who spoke no English and spent most of her life away from England. She had previously been Queen of Germany and Empress of the Holy Roman Empire, as her first husband was its Emperor Henri V (*d*. 1125) – hence her other title, Empress Matilda.
- ⚉ Henry II's most telling alternative title, apart from Curtmantle (French *court manteau*), was Henri Fitz-Empress, 'Henry, Son of the Empress'.
- ⚉ Henry (1133-89) was the first monarch to use, in his own lifetime, the title 'King of England', rather than 'King of the English'. To put this in context, he was also using the titles Duke of Normandy, Count of Anjou, Duke of Aquitaine, Duke of Gascony, Lord of Ireland and Count of Nantes, and was subservient, in the feudal scheme of things, to the King of France.

The records known to us as *The Anglo-Saxon Chronicle* famously comment that Stephen's nineteen-year reign was a time when 'Christ and his Saints slept':

In the days of this King there was nothing but strife, evil and robbery, for quickly the great men who were traitors rose against him. When the traitors saw that Stephen was a mild, good humoured man who inflicted no punishment, then they committed all manner of horrible crimes. They had done him homage and sworn oaths of fealty to him, but not one of their oaths was kept. They were all forsworn and their oaths broken. For every great man built him castles and held them against the King; they sorely burdened the unhappy people of the country with forced labour on the castles; and when the castles were built they filled them with devils and wicked men.

Henry II.

By night and by day they seized those they believed to have any wealth, whether they were men or women; and in order to get their gold or silver, they put them into prison and tortured them with unspeakable tortures, for never were martyrs tortured as they were. They hung them up by the feet and smoked them with foul smoke. They strung them up by the thumbs, or by the head, and hung coats of mail on their feet. They tied knotted cords round their heads and twisted it until it entered the brain. They put them in dungeons wherein were adders and snakes and toads and so destroyed them. Many thousands they starved to death.

I know not how to, nor am I able to tell of, all the atrocities nor all the cruelties which they wrought upon the unhappy people of this country. It lasted throughout the nineteen years that Stephen was King, and always grew worse and worse. Never did a country endure greater misery, and never did the heathen act more vilely than they did.

And so it lasted for nineteen long years while Stephen was King, till the land was all undone and darkened with such deeds and men said openly that Christ and his saints slept.

However, neither contender for the throne could rely on enough loyal support to guarantee outright victory and eventually Matilda was forced to return to Anjou and reconsider her battle plan. In 1153, Matilda and Henry Curtmantle were ready to resume the Anarchy, invading England with a host exceeding 3,000 men. Stephen was eventually forced to sign a truce with the Angevin invaders. His own son Eustace was bypassed in the succession in favour of Curtmantle (soon to be Henry II, first of the Plantagenet Kings). Stephen was allowed to remain on the throne, but he had little power now beyond the walls of his court. He died in 1154, and Henry II ascended to the throne with his wife, Eleanor of Aquitaine.

AD 1238

KILL THE POPE'S AMBASSADOR!

POPE GREGORY IX was not impressed. Certain scandals had been brought to his attention concerning the clergy and students of Oxford. Tucked away in their abbeys and seats of learning, there was rumoured to be more than a touch of the secular in the behaviour of the city's various tiers of holy men.

Since 1209, Rome had been watching Oxford closely, like an officer keeping tabs on a criminal out on parole. In that year, a student had accidentally shot and killed a townswoman. Instead of handing himself in, however, the student hid inside one of the University Halls. Three innocent scholars caught nearby were seized and hanged by the mob, and in response the entire University upped and left the city. The Pope himself sent a dictate which effectively closed down the institution for five years. This would have meant the end of the city's fortunes, so the bailiffs and principal citizens were forced to 'go to all the city churches with whips in their hands, barefooted, and in their shirts, and there pray the benefit of absolution'. They also had to pay a silver mark per year to the Hall, and entertain 100 poor scholars with a feast each year.

In 1214 the Pope gave the academic thumbs-up, and students began to return to the city. The office of Chancellor was created to oversee the general organisation and behaviour of students, and the practical aspects of curriculum, teaching and discipline were largely taken over by Black Friars and Grey Friars (Dominicans and Franciscans respectively). Friars, unlike society-shunning monks, carried out their religious vocation amongst the populace, making them ideal teachers (as well as doctors, and what we would now

A Dominican friar. (With kind permission of the Thomas Fisher Rare Book Library, University of Toronto)

A HISTORY OF OXFORD RIOTS

- ☠ In the 1220s the hard work of Chancellor Grossteste brought order and a new respectability to the restless University. But there were still many riots, as students and townsmen regularly battled it out. The year 1228 saw one of the bloodiest bouts, and there was another bloodbath in 1236.

- ☠ Jews were regularly attacked in Oxford. In 1268 a Jewish man was alleged to have insulted a Christian procession, and this was used as the basis for a pogrom.

- ☠ The traditional Town versus Gown bouts were far from over, though – there were rampages and deaths aplenty in the confrontations of 1252, 1274, 1298 and 1334; and a traditional punch-up on Bonfire Night in November was a fixture of the Oxford calendar until the late nineteenth century.

- ☠ After the 1334 punch-up a group of Oxford scholars ran away to Stamford, taking with them the brass sanctuary door-knocker from Brasenose College. The absconding students were ordered home, under threat of excommunication. Oxford grudges are long lasting: until the early 1800s, any man receiving an Oxford MA had to swear 'not to lecture in Stamford'. The door-knocker remained in a Stamford house named Brasenose Hall until 1890, when it was finally returned to Oxford.

Town vs Gown, still at war hundreds of years after the first Oxford riots.

Henry III.

term social workers). Indeed, the Grey Friars set up shop in St Ebbes, the poorest part of the city, something of a rubbish tip for the ill, leprous and generally down-and-out.

Then, in 1238, Cardinal Odo, the Papal Legate, came to stay at Osney Abbey. Oxford's Chancellor at the time, the highly devout Robert Grosseteste, world-renowned academic, philosopher and friend of Pope Gregory IX, had by then created a well-organised place of study finally able to rival Europe's great seat of learning, Paris, as the place to get the best education in the world.

Amongst Odo's retinue was his brother, who was overseeing the Osney kitchens due to his sibling's morbid fear of poisoning. The clerks (students) sent gifts of food; and one evening they made a solemn procession to Osney, arriving at the Guest's Hall. The porter who answered the door was one of the Cardinal's men, an Italian with no liking for the climate,

manners or gastronomy of the English. He asked who they were and what they wanted, with all the warmth of a night-club bouncer. Keeping his temper, the clerks' spokesman replied that they hoped to 'approach the presence of the Lord Legate and offer him their devoirs', i.e. their compliments and respects. The porter's reply could be translated roughly as 'sling your hooks'.

Patience evaporated, and the students shoved open the door. The Italian guards, in confusion, reached for their swords, but the clerks beat them senseless with fists and staves. Hearing the riot, Odo's brother, who was in the kitchens to prevent the pasta from being poisoned, took drastic action. Another clerk – an Irish chaplain, unrelated to the violent delegation and there simply to beg for food – had been annoying him beforehand, and the Italian chef answered his beggary by melting his face with scalding meat broth.

Unfortunately for the Italian, there was a witness, a Welsh clerk – and he was armed. 'Fie for shame, shall we suffer this?' He is said to have cried. Stringing his bow, the Welshman shot the guest chef. The Legate ran for his life, locking himself in the abbey church tower, while a message was sent to King Henry III, residing with his court at Abingdon Abbey. An armed guard arrived a few hours later to escort Odo away from the siege and into the presence of the very embarrassed King. Oxford University was effectively shut down once again, and grovelling letters of apology were sent to the Pope.

Oxford was back where it had been in 1209 – the future of the University was uncertain, and many scholars were forced to complete their studies at Salisbury and Northampton, or good old Paris. Some of the ringleaders of the riot were hunted down and arrested, some executed – and the report sent back to the Pope must have made interesting reading.

GRUMPY GREGORY AND FLYING FRANCIS: HOLY SUPERSTARS

Gregory IX was a victim of his own success. A late starter, he didn't want to be elected Pope, and yet followed a career path that led straight to the top. He was renowned as one of the age's most intelligent negotiators, combining great learning and intelligence with religious zeal and aristocratic manners and bearing.

At eighty-one, in the year 1227, Gregory was elected Pope, despite his protestations. He said he was too old, and unworthy. The latter claim, however, had been considerably undermined by a certain Francis of Assisi, who had prophesised that the reluctant Pope would become 'future bishop of all the universe'. Gregory was forced to bow to the will of the Church.

Francis himself was the son of a rich cloth merchant in Assisi, and had wielded weapons as a soldier. But the religious life swayed him from the usual path of death and debauchery, and he became one of the most revered saints in the history of the Christian Church. He was so holy that he would sometimes levitate in mid-meditation, allowing his followers to kiss his toes as they passed at chin-level. Francis was beatified just two years after his death in 1226.

St Francis, whose prophecy saw Gregory IX become Pope. (With kind permission of the Thomas Fisher Rare Book Library, University of Toronto)

THE REAL EDWARD II

EDWARD II (1284-1337), although hugely unpopular in England, was nonetheless a popular man in Oxford, having given money to Oxonian Adam de Brome to found Oriel College, the first University institution to receive royal patronage. Originally named The Hall of the Blessed Mary at Oxford, it was also known as King's Hall or College.

But John Deydras (aka John of Powderham, after the village of that name in Devon), an imaginative Oxford scholar with one ear missing, was not impressed by this show of royal wealth. In 1318 he announced that he was the rightful heir to the throne, and issued a proclamation to this effect. He then arrived at Oxford's royal seat, Beaumont Palace, asking for the keys to the door. As the King was not at home, he reasoned, it was a good time to move in. The Palace guards disagreed and Deydras was quickly arrested.

People assumed that this pretender was simply mad, which may indeed have been the case. But many agreed that he did resemble the King closely, and they were intrigued to know why he had only one ear.

Deydras' story was simple. As a royal toddler he had been playing under the not-very-watchful eye of his nurse in the courtyard at Beaumont Castle. A hungry sow had approached him and taken a bite; and the nurse, horrified to find that the heir to the throne had, whilst in her care, had his ear chewed off by a pig, took drastic action. She smuggled the bawling boy to a carter's house and swapped him for the carter's own son, who was the same age as the damaged heir.

John, the 'real' Edward, had a theory. The imposter King's wayward style of government and confused sexuality were all clues to the fact that he was the wrong man in the wrong place. Further clues could be found in Edward's love of peasant

Edward II.

28

THE BOCARDO – OBNOXIOUS TO THE ENEMY

This edifice, demolished in 1771, was part of the north gate of the city walls, near St Michael's church at the George Street end of Cornmarket.

The Bocardo was originally built for defensive purposes, flanked by twin towers and spanning the area between portcullised inner and outer gates. From this vantage point, according to seventeenth-century historian Anthony Wood, boiling water, oil 'or any other Weighty substance' could be poured on would-be attackers. It also featured 'a military engine… through which was cast down any Thing obnoxious to the Enemy approaching thereunto'.

The Bocardo, says Wood, was an impressive piece of defensive city wall: '…two great folding doors hung thereon, made strong with Bars of Iron nailed upon them; as also a massy Chain that crossed the outward Gate, by which we cannot otherwise imagine its primitive Beauty and Strength, not only for Fortifications, but for Battlements, Statues, and Arms thereon, which afforded Delight to Strangers that came that Way.'

When defending the city walls became a less day-to-day concern, some time after John Dreydas' imprisonment here in 1318, Wood says the mayor and bailiffs of Oxford converted the Bocardo into 'a common Prison for Debtors and Malefactors belonging to their own City… It has also been a Prison for Scholars for little Faults.'

Protestant Martyrs Cranmer, Latimer and Ridley were to be imprisoned in Oxford's Bocardo gaol.

From a combination of clues – an assumed British language derivation of *Buc* (elevation), *Ar* (near) and *Do* (junction), Trojan-Greek lion and eagle motifs on foundation stones, and the discovery in the foundations of an ancient Greek coin featuring the owl of Athena – some historians concluded that the Bocardo was a relic of the original city built by Trojan-descended mythical King Memphric in the second century BC.

In reality it was built in the eleventh century, either by Norman overlord Robert D'Oilly or a Saxon predecessor.

Left *St Michael's Saxon tower, the oldest building in Oxford.*

Below *Bocardo Gaol.*

activities such as digging, thatching, gardening and that most Oxfordian of pursuits, rowing. Confronted with this evidence and line of reasoning, many of Edward's enemies were keen to believe that he was indeed a changeling, the usual traits of royalty being so obviously absent.

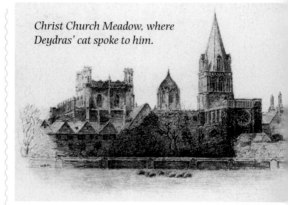

Christ Church Meadow, where Deydras' cat spoke to him.

To prove his point, Deydras offered to face the King in single combat. He was brought before the King in 1318 at Northampton. Edward greeted him with the words 'Welcome, my brother!', and, according to legend, offered him a job as court jester. But Queen Isabella felt terribly humiliated by the affair and failed to see the joke. When Deydras stood his ground and repeated his claims and challenge, he was sent to prison, charged with sedition.

Banged up in Oxford's Bocardo gaol, the pretender came to his senses and admitted that he had made up the story about the pig and the changeling. But he did himself no favours when he came up with something ever sillier. One day, he said, while walking across Christ Church Meadow, his pet cat had spoken to him. Revealing itself as the Devil in feline form, it sketched out the whole plan. The outcome was inevitable – both Deydras and his poor cat were hanged, and the man's body was burnt afterwards.

BEAUMONT PALACE

- This was built in 1130 by King Henry I as his *nova aula* (new hall), just beyond the north gate of the city. It was conveniently close to the Woodstock royal hunting lodge further north in the county.
- Woodstock's hunting lodge was upgraded to 'Palace' by Henry's grandson, Henry II. It had been finished in 1129, with the completion of an enclosing wall to mark the edge of the park and to pen the lions, leopards and other exotic animals that Henry I allowed to roam there.
- Kings Henry II, Richard I and John were all born at Beaumont.
- Edward I gave the Oxford palace to Italian lawyer, University lecturer and royal diplomat Francesco Accorsi in 1275.
- In 1318 Edward II gave it to God, in the form of Carmelite Friars, in thanks for his survival at the Battle of Bannockburn in 1314, in which the bloody territorial advances of his father had been reversed by Scottish King Robert the Bruce.
- Under Henry VIII the palace/friary, along with all other Catholic establishments, was dissolved. Beaumont was dismantled and its stones were used in the construction of Oxford Colleges Christ Church and St John's.
- The last remnants of the Oxford palace were levelled in 1829 when modern Beaumont Street was laid across this corner of the city.

WINING AND DYING IN OXFORD

ON 10 FEBRUARY 1355, University students Walter Spryngheuse and Roger de Chesterfield went to the Swindlestock Tavern at Carfax to spend a lazy afternoon. It was a Tuesday, and there were no lectures that day. They ordered wine (it being a general rule of thumb that taverns sold wine and inns sold beer), but found that it was not to their taste.

Hearing their complaints about the quality of his refreshments, taverner John de Bereford told them to shut up and drink up, or get out. The students opted for neither of these suggestions, insisting that the wine was bad and that Bereford should do something about it.

Stepping back briefly, it is worth underlining that then, as ever, students and townsfolk did not always get on well – to put it mildly. There had been a number of Town versus Gown riots prior to this altercation, and grievances had not been limited to irate letters to the press, as today, but had often ended in brawls and bloodshed.

As Spryngheuse cracked his foetid wine pot over John de Bereford's head, he can hardly have suspected that he was kick-starting the worst such riot in the city's history. The taverner was on the receiving end of a severe beating, and the students left the Swindlestock feeling very pleased with their hands-on approach to pub reviews.

THIS WAS THE SITE OF THE SWINDLESTOCK TAVERN 1250 – 1709

The town bailiffs confronted Spryngheuse and Chesterfield, demanding an apology and some form of compensation. The pair refused; and sensing a Town v. Gown incident to eclipse all others, Oxford's Mayor John de Bereford – yes, one and the same – licked his wounds and considered his limited options. He could not apprehend the men himself, as all members of the University were beyond his jurisdiction. So he wrote to the institution's Chancellor, John Charlton, requesting that the perpetrators be arrested. Charlton refused to comply.

The Mayor's friends then rang the bells of Carfax, the traditional call to arms for Oxford townsmen. In return, Spryngheuse and Chesterfield rang the bells of St Mary's on the High Street, a rallying call for students. The two impromptu armies pummelled each other; and, turning up to see what was afoot, Chancellor Charlton soon fled the bloody battle, doubtless wishing that he had taken a firmer stand against the trouble-making wine critics. As the sun went down the students congratulated themselves, having forced the townsmen to retreat.

UNIVERSITY CHALLENGE

Mayor de Bereford rode in person to Woodstock to ask King Edward III for assistance. Chancellor Charlton, meanwhile, ordered the students to make peace. Ignoring him, they blocked up the city gates, set fire to various buildings, looted several others, and attacked anyone who got in their way. The townsfolk responded by ambushing non-rioting students naively exercising in fields off St Giles. Eighty bowmen had gathered in St Giles' church, and now enjoyed target practice. Several students were shot dead.

Thinking that they had gone too far, the students were soon propelled into all-out war. Mayor de Bereford, having failed to win the support of the King, marched back to Oxford with an army of 2,000, gathered from the Oxfordshire countryside – men eager to make a historic tryst with the clerks of Oxenford. Chronicles record their war chant as 'Slay, slay! Havoc, havoc! Smite fast, give good knocks!' The armies met, but the students were relatively poorly armed and were soon fleeing. The Oxfordshire men pursued them, beating on the doors of the Halls and Colleges with the challenge: 'Bycheson cum forth!' – 'Come out, sons of bitches!'

On Thursday it was Chancellor Charlton who rode to Woodstock, and the pro-University King Edward promised reprisals. The events of that day did nothing to change his mind – fourteen University Halls were ransacked, many students were slaughtered, and many pulverised survivors were flung into prison. Some were scalped, apparently in mockery of the clerical tonsure (the shaven head associated with monks) that most of them had to wear. University Friars paraded with a cross to try and calm things down, but to no avail. As the sun went down on the third day of the riot, most students had been forced to flee Oxford, with others ducking

THE TOWN PENANCE

In a typically conservative footnote to the St Scholastica's Day Riot, the Mayor and dignitaries' humiliation was allowed to continue until 1825, and they paraded each year bare-headed to St Mary's to say prayers for the murdered men and pay their dues. In 1800 the Mayor decided to ignore the traditional demand – but the times were not yet a-changing, and the University sued him for an amount equivalent to the original fine imposed by Edward III. The event was symbolically laid to rest in 1955 at the 600-year commemorations, when the Chancellor was made a Freeman of the town, and the Mayor was given an Honorary Degree.

SWINDLESTOCK AND SCHOLASTICA

- ❧ The 1355 event has resonated through history partly on account of its assonance: two scholars swindled on St Scholastica's at Swindlestock.
- ❧ The saint in question was the sister of monastic founder St Benedict. She died in AD 543 and is buried in the proto-monastery at Monte Cassino, beside her more famous sibling.
- ❧ Swindlestock opened in 1250 and closed in 1709, by which time it had long been known as The Mermaid Tavern.
- ❧ Surviving tokens and bottles from the premises, marked with a distinctive mermaid motif, are exhibited in the Museum of Oxford.
- ❧ The site of the tavern is marked with a plaque, low down on the wall of Marygold House (currently occupied by Santander Bank).

behind the sturdy walls of Merton College, under siege.

King Edward brought the riot to a formal close, confiscating both Town and University Charters while he considered the evidence. He then ruled in favour of the Gown element, returning their charter and giving all students an instant pardon. This was to encourage them to return to the city, which was an important breeding ground for the country's political, religious and military masterminds, a resource that Edward was not willing to compromise, regardless of the rights and wrongs of the recent riot. Mayor John de Bereford was imprisoned.

To ram the message home, Oxford was forced to make a humiliating apology to the University, and to pay compensation plus a huge fine. Bereford was allowed out of gaol in order to sort out the practicalities of this. Each year on St Scholastica's Day, the Mayor and sixty-one Oxford dignitaries (one for each scholar killed in the riots) had to do penance by attending Mass in St Mary's church to pray for the souls of the dead students, and to pay a penny for every victim, the proceeds split between the University and the curate of St Mary's.

For the next few hundred years the University wielded all the power in the city, from controlling prices to regulating the drinks trade (how insufferable that must have made Spryngheuse and Chesterfield!), and from assessing taxes to confiscating weapons. As political victories go, it was pretty much complete.

Merton College.

RELIGION

A Martyr of Life and Death

THE RELIGIOUS MERRY-GO-ROUND of the sixteenth century produced many martyrs, with Tudors Henry, Edward, Mary and Elizabeth all sending their unfair share of unrepentant zealots to the noose and flames. Some of the most celebrated of these martyrs doused their fiery tempers in Oxford.

Thomas Cranmer, Archbishop of Canterbury, was chief architect of Henry VIII's divorce from his first wife Katherine of Aragon and his subsequent marriage to Anne Boleyn. Cranmer's involvement in this painful process steered his career path towards masterminding the biggest divorce of them all – the English Reformation, in which the country cast itself adrift after 900 years sailing on the See of Rome and set sail on the leaky ship The Church of England. Pragmatic Cranmer suggested that in this, and all other Church-related matters, Henry should ignore Rome and

Bishop Ridley.

In 1824, one John Sage of Oxford had something to say about pigs: he was sentenced to death for 'feloniously breaking open a house and stealing about 5 lbs. of bacon'.

seek advice from the wisest and most learned men in the land – i.e. the great and good of Oxford and Cambridge Universities. According to seventeenth-century historian Paul de Rapin, Henry agreed: 'He cried out in a transport of joy, I have got at last the right Sow by the ear!'

He did not have the sow for long: over the next few years, those who were not willing to close their eyes and follow their snout were sent to their deaths. Chancellor Thomas More and Bishop of Rochester John Fisher were the first high-profile martyrs, refusing to take the oath that

THE DEATHS OF LATIMER AND RIDLEY

Foxe's Book of Martyrs records the sad story of the deaths of Ridley and Latimer.

'On the north side of the town, in a ditch over against Baliol-College, the place of execution was appointed... and when everything was in readiness, the prisoners were brought forth by the mayor and bailiffs.

'Dr Ridley had on a black gown furred and faced with foins, such as he used to wear when he was a bishop; a tippet of velvet, furred, likewise about his neck, a velvet night-cap upon his head, with a corner cap, and slippers on his feet. He walked to the stake between the mayor and the aldermen &c.

'After him came Mr Latimer, in a poor Bristol frieze frock much worn, with his button cap and kerchief on his head, all ready to the fire, a new and long shroud hanging down to his feet...

'Dr Ridley, looking back, saw Mr Latimer coming after. Unto whom he said, 'Oh, are you there?'-'Yea,' said Mr Latimer, 'have after, as fast as I can.' So he followed at a distance till they came to the stake.

...Mr Latimer quietly suffered his keeper to pull off his hose, and his other apparel, which was very simple; and being stripped to his shroud, he seemed as comely a person as one could well see.

Then Dr Ridley, standing as yet in his trousers, said to his brother, 'It were best for me to go in my trousers still.' 'No,' said Mr Latimer, 'it will put you to more pain: and it will do a poor man good.' Whereunto Dr Ridley said, 'Be it in the name of God,' and so unlaced himself.

...The smith then took a chain of iron, and brought it about their middles: and as he was knocking in the staple, Dr Ridley took the chain in his hand and said, 'Good fellow, knock it in hard, for the flesh will have its course.' Then Mr Shipside brought him a bag of gunpowder, and tied it about his neck [and about the Doctor's neck too].

Then they brought a lighted fagot and laid it at Dr Ridley's feet... When Dr Ridley saw the fire flaming up towards him, he cried out, 'Into thy hands, Lord, I commend my spirit' ... Mr Latimer, on the other side, cried as vehemently, 'O Father of Heaven, receive my soul.' After which he soon died, seemingly with little pain.

But Dr Ridley, from the ill-making of the fire, the fagots being green, and piled too high, so that the flames being kept down by the green wood, burned fiercely underneath, was put to such exquisite pain, that he desired them for God's sake, to let the fire come unto him; which his brother-in-law hearing, but not very well understanding, to rid him of his pain, heaped fagots upon him, so that he quite covered him, and made the fire so vehement beneath, that it burned all his nether parts before it touched the upper, and made him struggle under the fagots, and often desire to let the fire come to him, saying, 'I cannot burn'...

In which pains he laboured until one of the bystanders, with his bill, pulled the fagots from above, and where he saw the fire flame up, he wrestled himself to that side. And when the fire touched the gunpowder, he was seen to stir no more, but burned on the other side, falling down at Mr Latimer's feet; his body being divided.'

The site of the martyr's imprisonment.

...putting off his garment, he prepared himself for death. His shirt was made long down to his feet. His feet were bare; likewise his head, when both his caps were off, was so bare that not one hair could be seen upon it. His beard was so long and thick, that it covered his face with marvellous gravity.

When the fire was lit, therefore, he declared, 'This is the hand that wrote it [the recantation], and therefore shall it suffer first punishment'. As the fire mounted, Cranmer allowed his right hand to burn. Sources say he cried out, 'This hand hath offended!', or 'This unworthy right hand!', throughout the ordeal.

The Oxford Martyrs' Memorial stands on St Giles in Oxford, but the actual burnings took place on Broad Street. The alleged spot (in the former town ditch) is marked with a cross on the road.

placed Henry VIII as head of the newly established Anglican Church.

But when Henry's Catholic daughter, Mary I, took power, it was the Anglicans turn to suffer. Bishops Hugh Latimer and Nicholas Ridley went to the flames first, Ridley reassuring his friend that God would either lessen the agony of the flames, or bolster their spirits to withstand the pain. Latimer replied: 'Be of good cheer, Ridley, and play the man. We shall this day, by God's grace, light up such a candle in England as I trust will never be put out.'

However, it was Cranmer's death in March 1556, at the age of sixty-seven, that would produce the most striking image for local legend. Cranmer had tried to save his own life by signing a recantation, after being tormented with 'every engine that could be thought of ... to shake his constancy', and spending time in 'the most loathsome part of the prison in which he had been confined, [where they] treated him with unparalleled severity'. But his recantation was to no avail: he too came to the spot were Ridley and Latimer perished.

The horrible death of Cranmer, as depicted in Foxe's Book of Martyrs.

TEN REASONS TO BE HANGED, DRAWN AND QUARTERED

Out went Mary, and in came Henry's younger daughter, Protestant-with-a-grudge Elizabeth I. In 1581 Edmund Campion, a leading recusant (a term for die-hard Catholics), was unearthed in hidden chambers at Lyford Grange Manor in Oxfordshire, along with fellow priests. He had fled here from another recusant stronghold at Stonor Park in the same county.

Campion had lived in various bits of Catholic Europe throughout the 1570s and came back to England as a Jesuit missionary, masquerading as a jewel merchant. At Stonor Park he printed and distributed Catholic tracts, 400 copies of his *Ten Reasons* (arguments against Anglicanism) turning up on the pews of St Mary's in Oxford one Sunday morning in 1581. He was already known as the mastermind behind the mission, and would make the perfect scapegoat in Oxfordshire, a county renowned as a hotbed of closet Catholicism.

The captured Campion was driven through Oxford, where he was greeted by many as a hero. He was a Fellow of St John's College, and had led a debate here in front of Elizabeth in happier times. She had, indeed, voiced her high regard for the man, who had first found favour under

Broad Street, St Giles.

Queen Mary. But the former affections of Elizabeth and the University were not enough to save him. He was tried, tortured, hanged, drawn and quartered at Tyburn.

Edward Campion and the two priests arrested with him at Lyford – Thomas Ford and John Colleton – are commemorated annually with a Mass at Lyford. In 1970 Campion's long spiritual journey was completed when he was made a saint by the Roman Catholic Church. Some of the others got there earlier – Thomas Ford was beatified in 1889, and Thomas More and John Fisher were given the holy thumbs-up in 1935, on the 400th anniversary of their deaths.

THE MARTYRS' MEMORIAL

Martyrs' Memorial.

☠ Cranmer, Latimer and Ridley are the subjects of George Gilbert Scott's Martyrs' Memorial on St Giles in Oxford, completed in 1843. In 1830s Oxford the principles for which they had died were judged to be under threat. Catholic emancipation was a reality, its mainspring being Oxonian Cardinal John Henry Newman's 'Oxford Movement'. The Memorial was a reaction against this trend, and was very controversial at the time.

☠ Its inscription, originally circulated as part of the money-raising effort, mentions the Anglican martyrs and 'the sacred truths which they had affirmed and maintained against the errors of the Church of Rome' – a direct swipe at Cardinal Newman and his allies.

☠ A.W.N. Pugin, a giant in architecture compared with the relatively unheard of Gilbert, and father of the Victorian Gothic revival, wrote of the 'atrocities' committed by the so-called martyrs against Catholics. He described the proposed memorial as a puny construction in a city 'which owes its very existence to Catholic piety'.

☠ The project went ahead regardless, in spite of shortfalls in funding. Its committee had to borrow £250 from the parish of St Mary Magdalen, of which £200 is still outstanding, theoretically. £9,333 16s 4½d was the final cost of the folly, and Gilbert was magnanimous enough to forgo part of his fee due to lack of funds. The restoration work of 2003 cost considerably more.

☠ The Memorial is the object of a traditional practical joke, in which visitors to the city are told that the spire-like monument is actually the top of a subterranean church. The 'access point' is a set of steps leading down to St Giles' public toilets.

AD 1577

BLACK ASSIZE
AND BLACK DEATH

GAOL FEVER WAS a common cause of sickness and death in the dungeons of Olde England. Once present, it was difficult to contain. Oxford has experienced several outbreaks, but the most drastic was in 1577 when Rowland Jenkes, bookseller, faced his accusers in the Shire Hall (on the site of the modern County Hall on New Street) at an event later known as the Black Assize. Jenkes was charged with selling seditious material – in this case books whose pro-Catholic contents questioned the legitimacy of the ruling Protestant status quo under Queen Elizabeth I.

Found guilty, Jenkes was sentenced to be nailed by the ears to the castle pillory. Rumour soon spread that he had placed a curse on his accusers during this ordeal, for between 6 July and 12 August two judges, the coroner and several jurors from the Black Assize died from gaol fever, along with others in Oxford totalling 300, and an alleged 200 more in the surrounding county. An alternative rumour whispered that Jenkes had concocted a poisonous candle and secretly set it smouldering during the proceedings, the most malicious aromatherapy ever recorded.

One chronicler wrote: 'The Court were surprised with a pestilent savour, whether arising from the noisome smell of the prisoners, or from the damp of the ground, is uncertain; but all that were present, within forty hours died, except the prisoners, and the women and children; and the contagion went no farther.' Another added: 'Above 100 Scholars, besides Townsmen, were seized with a strange Distemper, and ran about the streets like Madmen, and beat their Governors'.

Examining the case with an enlightened modern eye, the fact that the Shire Hall was filled with pestilent prisoners from the castle gaol would seem to be the obvious starting point when looking for a scientific explanation. Like many other inmates of damp and unhygienic institutions, Jenkes and co. were infested with lice, whose faeces can carry *Rickettsia prowazekii*, better known as Epidemic Typhus; although another theory proposes that the fever was in fact a new blooming of the rat-flea-borne plague that had hit the city in 1571.

The outbreak ended abruptly on 12 August. The detail concerning the immunity of prisoners, women and children is tantalising. It certainly gave popular credence to the theories of a curse; and the statistic may indeed have been invented to back up the theory.

A plaque erected outside the County Hall in 1875 reads: 'Near this spot stood the ancient Shire Hall, unhappily famous in history as the scene in July 1577 of the Black Assize, when a malignant disease known as Gaol Fever caused the death

Oxford Castle: a pleasant view of a breeding ground for a deadly epidemic.

JAIL-HOUSE ROT

- Francis Bacon, in his *Natural History for the Building up of Philosophy*, 1609, wrote about gaol fever. It was thought at the time to originate in the foul odours of damp, pestilential air: 'The most pernicious infection next to the plague is the smell of the gaol, where prisoners have been long and close and nastily kept whereof we have had in our time experience twice or thrice, when both the judges, that sat upon the gaol, and numbers of those, that attended the business, or were present, sickened upon it, and died. Therefore it were good wisdom, that in such cases the gaol were aired before they be brought forth.'
- Typhus in the United Kingdom was still raging in the nineteenth century. It became known as 'Irish Fever' due to its devastations during the Irish famine of 1846-9, in which it killed 100,000 people. This 'Irish' strain spread to England via immigration.
- Other biting parasites can transmit epidemic typhus too – including the self-same rat flea that carries 'Black Death' plague.
- The first vaccine was developed in the inter-war period of the twentieth century by Polish biologist Rudolf Stefan Weigl, with more effective ones appearing in the 1940s. DDT was widely used to spray people at risk (including soldiers), although that chemical proved to be a wolf in sheep's clothing, causing its own brand of chaos in the environment. In spite of all this, many poorer areas of the world are still ravaged by epidemic typhus.
- Typhus is not to be confused with typhoid fever, yet another of the old-fashioned gaol's many health hazards. This is a water-borne disease (similar to cholera) caused by the bacterium *Salmonella enterica*, transmitted via food or water contaminated with the faeces of an infected person.

PLAGUED BY VERMIN

- The Black Death is thought (in spite of frequent alternative theories) to have been caused by the bacteria *Yersinia pestis*, multiplying in the guts of the globe-trotting Oriental rat flea (*Xenopsylla cheopis*) that infested the black rat (*Rattus rattus*), amongst other hairy hosts.
- The first *Yersinia pestis* to infest a flea's innards lived in China, its kindred travelling the Silk Road to reach Europe via the Crimea in 1346. Passenger ships and their rats transported the plague to every city on the map in a terrifyingly short time.
- The economic and political chaos that followed as a direct result of plague mortality has been blamed for most of the human upheavals of the 200 years following the first outbreak.
- 1665 saw England's last outbreaks, although plague did not die out in Europe until the nineteenth century.
- Modern antibiotics can reduce mortality rates to 1 per cent; but, if untreated, bubonic plague can still wipe out up to 90 per cent of its victims.

Gloucester Green Cattle market at its height, from a photograph in the Museum of Oxford. The college that used to stand here closed after all of its students died of plague. (Museum of Oxford)

within forty days of the Lord Chief Baron of the Exchequer, Sir Robert Bell, the Lord High Sheriff (Sir Robert D'Oyly of Merton) and about three hundred more. The malady from the stench of the Prisoners developed itself during the Trial of one Rowland Jenkes, a saucy foul-mouthed Bookseller, for scandalous words uttered against the Queen'.

FROM PLAGUE PIT TO COLLEGE

In the disease-ridden annals of Oxford, the devastations of the Black Assize epidemic are trumped only by the Black Death of 1348. Deaths were an everyday occurrence while this first ever outbreak of the plague

Entrance to New College. The institution was built on top of a plague mound

raged in and around the city, and many of the ancient University Halls stood empty afterwards, all their students dead. One such institution, Gloucester Hall, closed its doors forever in 1348 and only lingers as the basis of the name Gloucester Green, site of the modern bus station and former cattle market.

The Black Death lasted from November 1348 until June the following year. Seventeenth-century historian Anthony Wood states that at the peak of the pestilence up to sixteen bodies a day were buried in a single churchyard. A third of the population of the city is thought to have perished, and the outbreak is a key factor in the decline of Oxford over the decades that followed – especially as further outbreaks occurred every two or three years, on average, over the next 150 years. With less people around there were less rents being paid, and less trade and money in general – always a recipe for urban decline.

The most vivid illustration of these grimmest of times can be found in the comments of a jury of 1378, deciding whether to give the go-ahead for the development of 13 acres of non-prime real estate in the north-east corner of Oxford. The land had no buildings or enclosures of any kind, boasting only an all-purpose dump for sewage, rubbish and, when an outbreak caused a logjam of bodies, plague victim's corpses. The only people to frequent the spot were criminals, prostitutes and their seedy clients. Something had to be done, the jurors concurred, and gave planning permission to Chancellor of England (and Bishop of Winchester) William of Wykeham. On these unpromising foundations, New College was born. The 'plague mound' can still be seen in the College grounds.

THE SIEGES OF OXFORD

THE ENGLISH CIVIL War had relatively little long-lasting physical impact on Oxford (apart from the levelling of its castle), but during the years of conflict the city changed its personality as alarmingly as Jekyll transforming into Hyde. Swapping its academic robes for the trappings of war, Oxford became a mirror for England, with schools turned overnight into munitions dumps, students ousted by soldiers, and flocks in the surrounding fields displaced by cannons.

It was one of the few times in history when royal approval was bad, bad news. With the University predominantly pro-Royalist, King Charles I had chosen Oxford as his base of operations in 1643. His court and parliament installed itself at Christ Church, while his Queen Henrietta Maria's huge retinue inflicted itself on Merton. Their sons Charles and James, and nephews Prince Rupert and Prince Maurice, installed their households in the city too, with the symbolic assent of pro-Royalist University Chancellor Archbishop Laud (who was imprisoned in the Tower of London at the time).

New College was transformed into an army warehouse of munitions and hardware, while Oriel became a foundry, producing cannons, and also housing the King's Privy Council. The mill at Osney ground gunpowder instead of flour. New Inn Hall became the Oxford Mint, churning out coinage to pay the army, using melted down College plate and other metal ware purloined from University and household alike. The new University schools became stores for foodstuffs and workshops for clothing and other necessities. To make matters worse, the inhabitants of Oxford were heavily taxed to finance the King's military takeover; all men aged between sixteen and forty-five were forced to enlist in the army; and, as if to symbolise the general wretchedness of the city in its warlike guise, a gibbet was erected in its

Ruins of Osney Abbey, near the mill, at the time of the King's stay.

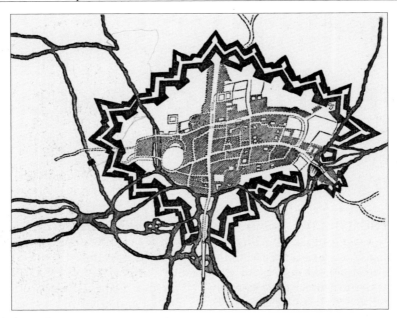

Plan of proposed defences for the Siege of Oxford. They were never built.

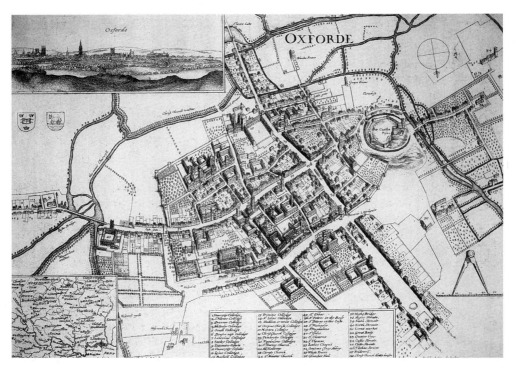

Oxford at the time of the conflict. (With kind permission of the Thomas Fisher Rare Book Library, University of Toronto)

centre at Carfax. The plague that proceeded to rage through the populace simply added insult to injury.

The University staggered on, with reduced numbers of students and Masters, and with a much patchier curriculum than usual. In a show of appeasement honorary degrees were handed out to Charles' sons Charles and James (both to do stints on the throne in the Restoration era to come), to make the loyalist, Royalist message loud and clear.

But this veneer was easy to crack. Those pesky Parliamentarians and their Roundhead army had a base at Abingdon, just over 7 miles away, and Oxford was a priority target: one killer raid and the whole thing would soon be over, with the King captured and his headquarters seized.

The first attempt duly came in May 1644, when Roundhead commanders William Waller and Edmund Ludlow sketched out plans for the first siege of Oxford. On 27 May Waller made his move; but the advance was comfortably crushed by Royalist dragoons near Newbridge. Undeterred, Earl of Essex Robert Devereaux paraded his Parliamentarian army just north of Oxford, crossing the river at Sandford Ferry and viewing the city's walls and defences from the vantage point of Bullingdon Green. A contingent of horsemen made a quick raid on the eastern edge of the city, just to let it know that a siege was something the townsfolk ought to be worried about. There were minor skirmishes at Headington Hill and St Clements, where cannon were fired at the invaders while King Charles watched from Magdalen bell tower. The cheeky riders escaped back to Essex's main host, which rode to Islip, 7 miles north of the city centre, and made camp there.

By June the Parliamentarians were ready to begin the siege proper. The Royalists, having attempted to consolidate their position by abandoning bases at

William Waller. (With kind permission of the Thomas Fisher Rare Book Library, University of Toronto)

Woodstock and elsewhere in the vicinity and gathering their full force in Oxford, nevertheless feared that they were no match for the massive enemy army. More to the point, they only had provisions to last fourteen days. This vital issue of food supply was, as is so often the case in sieges, the deciding factor.

So, while a big chunk of Royalist army heaved its cannon and arms towards Abingdon as a diversion, Charles made hasty arrangements with his Privy Council for general tactics during his proposed absence; and then, gathering his retinue after an agreed signal of trumpet blasts, he fled from Oxford disguised as his sons' tutor's servant, at 9 p.m. on 3 June. The exodus included Prince Charles, a gaggle of courtiers, 2,500 musketeers, and all the Royalist cavalry. They flitted through Wolvercote, making it to Burford and relative safety seventeen hours later.

OXFORDSHIRE: HAUNTED BY WAR

—∞∞∞—

Oxford was not the only place in the county to suffer the guns and 'grenados' of the Civil War:

- During 1643 Royalist Prince Rupert had harried Parliamentarian garrisons at Chinnor and Postcombe, razing the villages. On 18 June he tiptoed to Chalgrove to lay an ambush for the pursuing enemy. The ploy failed, but in typical derring-do mode he switched to Plan B, leaping over the hedge that separated the two forces to lead his men into battle, and on to victory at the Battle of Chalgrove Field. It was the kind of stuff that brought him fame, short-lived though his star proved to be.
- Parliamentarian commander John Hampden had a less successful day at Chalgrove. He levelled his pistol at the enemy and the weapon exploded in his hand, mortally wounding him.
- The Royalists had occupied Culham Bridge as part of their Abingdon encampment. In 1644 Oliver Cromwell's men took it as a base from which to attack Royalist supply lines to Oxford. At the Battle of Culham Bridge on 11 January 1645 Royalist commander Sir Henry Gage died of injuries inflicted during his failed attempt to recapture and destroy the bridge.
- 'Site of the Battle of Cropredy Bridge. From Civil War deliver us', reads a plaque on the bridge in the village of Cropredy. The Battle took place on 29 June 1644, William Waller's Parliamentarians suffering heavy losses; but the conflict ended with no clear winner.
- Prince Rupert, key general in many of the early Royalist campaigns, can still be seen on New College Lane in Oxford, where he and his entire cavalry race off in ghostly form to their confrontation at Chalgrove on the anniversary of the battle. Less reliable are the witnesses who claim to have seen King Charles and Archbishop Laud playing bowls with their severed heads in St John's College Library.

—∞∞∞—

ALL IS FAIRFAX IN LOVE AND WAR

The King's absence was not immediately obvious to his enemies. In addition to his Abingdon decoy, Charles had left 3,500 infantry in North Oxford, their cannon trained on the besiegers. There was also a surprising lack of communication and vigilance (and evidently some very poor eyesight, given the size of the royal exodus) from Essex and William Waller, who had stationed troops east and north of the city. These factors, plus a small dose of good luck, smuggled the main man safely away from the action.

Waller, in a flurry of bolting horses and slamming stable doors, eventually saw through the ruse and hurtled after the King's train, managing to cut down a few Royalists at Burford. But Charles hadn't paused, and was soon safe in Royalist Worcester. The sound of Parliamentarians kicking themselves echoed through Oxfordshire. As a communication between Royalist bigwigs Lord Digby and Prince Rupert put it, 'If Essex and Waller had either jointly pursued us, or attacked Oxford, all had been lost'.

Essex and Waller were taken off duty, and Sergeant-Major General Browne was put in charge of the Oxford siege-in-

Prince Rupert, Charles I's nephew, a soldier famous for his feats of valour, defended Oxford during the attacks. (With kind permission of the Thomas Fisher Rare Book Library, University of Toronto)

waiting. His mission was to 'reduce' not just Oxford, but Banbury and Wallingford too. His men took several potshots at the city, but Browne held back his major campaign until the New Year, when the New Model Army (established partly on the recommendation of William Waller) declared the seizure of Oxford its number-one priority. Oliver Cromwell and General Browne were stationed just beyond the city walls, and Prince Rupert, former scourge of the Parliamentarians, was thwarted in his intended approach to Oxford. On 23 May 1645 the committee of the army was given the go-ahead by the House of Commons to raise 'such money and necessaries for the Siege of Oxford'. Thomas Fairfax, Parliamentarian General, picked up money and weapons of mass destruction at Windsor (including 500 barrels of gunpowder, 30 tons of bullets, and various 'grenado shells' and 'hand grenades').

On 21 May Fairfax blocked up all routes of escape, and Oxford was under siege again, its opposing forces occupying different suburbs. River crossings were guarded, all outlying houses were commandeered, and the Royalists torched a few houses in their retreat to Wolvercote in the north of the city. Fairfax watched from the frontline, literally dodging bullets on one occasion, while in a show of strength his cannons proved how far they could penetrate the enemy ranks when a ball was fired from Marston to the walls of Christ Church a mile away.

Oxford mounted an impressive, desperate defence on 2 June. Just before sunrise Royalist horse and footmen made a surprise attack on Headington Hill, killing fifty of Fairfax's besiegers, wounding many more and taking ninety-six prisoners. Many thought this would simply encourage the Parliamentarians to finish the job. But Fairfax amazed everyone by arranging an exchange of prisoners and calling off the siege, pointing out that the King, their main enemy, had fled long ago with his chief generals, and that even now he was gathering strength in alternative strongholds. Oxford, Fairfax argued, was a diversion. He would not waste his time in labour-intensive siege warfare again.

Well, not until the following year...

AD 1642-5

ANTHONY WOOD

Eye-Witness to War

HISTORIAN ANTHONY WOOD wrote an eye-witness account of the Civil War and its effects on his upbringing in and around Oxford. He begins his narrative of these years by writing proudly of elder brother Thomas' Royalist bravado – indicative of the strong loyalty of the University to King Charles I.

> 23 October 1642... The great Fight at Edgehill in Warwickshire called Keynton-Battle, between the Armies of Ch.I and his Parliament was began. Upon the first news at Oxon. that the Armies were going to fight, Mr. Wood's eldest brother Thomas left his Gown at the Town's end, ran to Edgehill, did his Majesty good service, returned on horse-back well accoutred and afterwards was made an Officer in the King's Army.

Royalist the city may have been, but not everyone was overjoyed at Charles' decision to base himself in Oxford. In November the King had commandeered the city, storing his ammunition and hardware in New College's Tower and cloister. This meant the Master and scholars had to relocate 'to the Choristers Chamber at the East end of the Common Hall of the said College. It was then a dark nasty room, and very unfit for such a purpose, which made the Scholars often complain, but in vain.'

Even the Royalist Wood family found good cause for complaint. They were forced out of their house near Merton College to make way for John Lord Cole, Master of the Rolls, who had requisitioned it. Wood says his father 'moved to a little house in his Backside, which he about 2 or 3 years before had new built'. But the stress of the Backside move sent Wood's father into decline, and a few weeks later he died:

New College Lane.

Robert, Earl of Essex on horseback. (With kind permission of the Thomas Fisher Rare Book Library, University of Toronto)

...in the room over the kitchen: and being a fat corpulent man, and therefore his Body would not keep, he was buried... on the same day... It was much lamented... that A.W. [he always refers to himself in the third person] and his brother Christopher were left young when their Father died, and that nobody was left (because of the Civil War) to take care of them, only a woman [i.e. their mother].

Wood also complains that the family silver was seized by the King's men, along with all the other plate in Oxford (which is why very little pre-war College silver survives), to turn into coins at the hastily installed Oxford Mint.

Oxford, although occupied by the Royalist army and the various royal courts, was far from being an impregnable fortress. There was widespread fear that the Parliamentarians would besiege the city at some point. 'The Rebels', as Wood labels them, were allowed to pass by the borders without any attempt being made to repel them. He notes how, in 1643, Robert, Earl of Essex, 'Generalissimo of the Parliament Forces', came from one of his strongholds, Abingdon, over Sandford Ferry on his way to nearby Islip. As his host came close to the city walls, Wood says Essex and his generals 'faced the City of Oxon. for several hours, whilst their carriages slipped away behind them. This gave some terror to the Garrison of Oxon. his Majesty being then therein, and great talk there was, that a siege would suddenly follow'.

Wood's mother was pretty certain of this, and she sent Anthony and Christopher 'with an horse and man into the country: And because the Infection [plague] was then in Oxon. she ordered, that they should be conveyed to Tetworth, 10 miles distant from Oxford... There they continued till it was through, that they had no infection about them, and then they were conveyed... to a market town called Thame.'

THAME GOES WILD

'While A. Wood and his brother Christopher continued at Thame,' wrote the diarist, 'you cannot imagine what great disturbances they suffered by the Soldiers of both parties, sometimes by the Parliament soldiers of Aylesbury, sometimes by the King's from Borstall house, and sometimes from the King's at Oxon. and at Wallingford.'

Wood tells of Royalist Colonel Thomas Blagge, Governor of Wallingford, retreating on horseback from a skirmish at Long Crendon via Thame, passing by the house where the young historian was staying. Fifty Parliamentarians were in hot pursuit: Blagge raced by, his face all cut and bloodied; and one of his men, heading up

SUNDAY LUNCH IS OVERCOOKED

The greatest damage inflicted on the city during this period of uncertainty and Civil War came not from the sparring armies, but from a Sunday roast. The fire which followed took out a large chunk of city where modern George Street, New Hall Inn Lane and Queen Street now stand. According to Wood:

> On Sunday the 8th of October happened a dreadful fire in Oxon. such a one (for the shortness of the time wherein it burned) that all the Ages before could hardly parallel. It began about two of the clock in the afternoon in a little poor house on the south side of Thames Street (leading from the North gate to High Bridge) occasioned by a Foot-Soldier's roasting a pig, which he had stolen. The wind being very high, and in the north, blew the flames southward and very quick and strangely, and burnt all houses and stables (except St Marie's College) standing between the back-part of those houses, that extend from the North Gate to St Martin's Church on the east, and those houses in the North Baylie called New Inn Lane, on the west: then all the old houses in the Bocardo (with the Bocardo itself) [the old city prison] which stood between St Martin's Church and the Church of St Peter in the Baylie; among which were two which belonged to A. Wood's mother... to her great loss, and so consequently to the loss of her sons.

the sloping bank opposite Wood's door, was thrown by his panicking horse. One of the enemy aimed a pistol at him,

> ...but the trooper crying Quarter, the Rebels came up, rifled him, and took him and his horse away with them. Crafford [Colonel, and Governor of the Aylesbury Garrison] rode on without touching him, and ever or anon he would be discharging his pistol at some of the fag-end of Blagge's horse, who rode thro the West end of Thame... towards Ricot.

Crafford ended the pursuit here, opting for a few swift drinks in a local inn instead.

Wood says he later watched Royalist Captain Bunce attack the forces of Captain Phips at 'the Bridge below Thame Mill':

> ...this valiant Captain Bunce, after he had received a volley from Phips and his partie (which touched only one common soldier slightly) charged over the Bridge, and

with his pistols shot one of them dead, and beat them off the bridge so as they all ran away, but lost just half their number: for besides him that was killed there were none taken, whereof two were Captain Phips himself and his Lieutenant, ten only escaping, most of which had marks bestowed on them.

DEBAUCHED BY BEARING ARMS

Wood's third encounter with the cut and thrust of war was on 7 September 1645, when William Legge, Royalist Governor of Oxford, led 400 horsemen and 60 musketeers from the city with his brother, High Sheriff of Oxfordshire David Walter. The mustering was so sudden, and so early, that some men were said to have ridden forth in their nightshirts. They stormed the 'rebels' at Thame, breaking down their barricades; and, 'this done, the two gallant majors charged the Rebels up thro the Street, doing execution all the way to the Market-place, where... (they) gave the Rebels such a charge as made them fly out of the Town'.

The town and its stables were searched thoroughly for the enemy, and a few hundred horses and prisoners were marched out of town that evening. The regrouped rebels attacked the Royalists as they made their way back to Oxford, killing a few in the process.

There was not to be much more good news for the Oxford Royalists. Wood writes:

Wednesday and Midsomer day, the Garrison of Oxon which was the chiefest hold the King had, and wherein he had mostly resided while the Civil War continued, was surrendered for the use of the Parliament, as most of his Garrisons were this year, occasioned by the fatal Battle of Naseby, which happened in the last year, wherein the King and his party were in a woeful manner worsted. In the evening of the said Day, many of the King's Foot-party, that belonged to the Oxon Garrison, came into Thame, and laid down their armes there, being then a wet season...

After his return to the house of his Nativity, [Wood] found Oxford empty, as to Scholars, but pretty well replenished with Parliamentarian Soldiers. Many of the Inhabitants had gained great store of wealth from the Court and Royalists, that had for several years continued among them; but as for the young men of the City and University, he found many of them to have been debauched by bearing arms, and doing the duties belonging to soldiers, as watching, warding, and sitting in Tippling-Houses for whole nights together.

WE SURRENDER!

IN NOVEMBER 1645, in the absence of a decisive blow from either side in the Civil War, King Charles I decided to spend another winter in Oxford. The city had lost none of its Royalist military trappings in the intervening months, but this time the Parliamentarians were firmly entrenched too, their military mastermind Thomas Fairfax installed in the homely surroundings of 17 Mill Lane, Marston. Now known as 'Cromwell House', the building was indeed visited by the war's most famous beneficiary, Oliver, in 1646 as the conflict reached its crucial final stages. It was also the scene of negotiations over the long-drawn out Treaty of Oxford.

When Charles arrived on 5 November (traditional day for annual Town versus Gown battles, appropriately), his cause was very much on the wane. Prince Rupert had been routed after the Battle of Marston Moor near York on 2 July 1644, and was much out of favour with the King, so his hopes now rested on reinforcements. A legion of Welsh Royalist conscripts gathering for rendezvous in Worcester, and an army of Scots loyal to the old Stuart dynasty, played a key role in Charles' increasingly desperate remedies.

The first part of the plan – the Welsh and Worcester reinforcements – came a cropper when their General, Lord Astley, was defeated and captured at Stow-on-the-Wold on 21 March, his bolstered army scattered. Charles, realising that he was now a prisoner in his own city, made a second plan to flee Oxford in disguise. With Worcester no longer a Royalist safety zone his plan was to travel to the coast and make his way by sea to Montrose in Scotland.

Meanwhile, the New Model Army was ordered to 'straiten' Oxford. Various bits of strategic Oxfordshire and Berkshire were stuffed with soldiers, and several skirmishes took place. Gunpowder was delivered to the Parliamentarians from their long-

Oliver Cromwell.

Charles I twice fled Oxford. His first stay was very unpopular with New College, whose Master and scholars were forced to stay in a 'dark nasty room'. (With kind permission of the Thomas Fisher Rare Book Library, University of Toronto)

beaten back with surprising ease, and many of their scaling ladders – essential for getting over the walls – were captured. More than a hundred of Rainsborough's men were killed in the battle, and many more were wounded. But the Woodstock siege continued, and on 26 April the Manor House fell to the Parliamentarians, its governor and his army fleeing to Oxford, weaponless. Rainsborough himself met his end in 1648 at the siege of Pontefract, when Royalists tried to kidnap him and use him as a bargaining tool but accidentally killed him in the process.

Charles, meanwhile, was preparing to don the disguise and scarper. His men at the Oxford Mint managed to forge Thomas Fairfax's official seal, and using this token Charles made it as far as London, adopting the on-the-road name 'Harry'. This was possibly a sentimental reference to Shakespeare's play *Henry V*, in which Prince Harry, in disguise, tours the English army's encampment before rallying his men to victory at Agincourt.

A letter from Parliamentarian commander Colonel Payne on 29 April revealed: 'News is confirmed by all that come from Oxford that he went out disguised in a Montero [a soldier's cap] with a hat upon it.' It was another audacious escape; but the hoped-for rallying and re-invasion from Scotland was not to be.

On 1 May Thomas Fairfax sent in the army. He had spied on the Royalist defences and artillery in the University Parks from a vantage point on the top of St Nicholas' church in Marston, so he knew exactly what to expect. His army occupied all key villages around the city, establishing his HQ at Headington. Faringdon, Radcot, Wallingford and Boarstall House were blockaded to prevent them drip-feeding reinforcements to the Oxford Royalists. Three thousand men were stationed at Headington Hill, with further contingents at Cowley, Elsfield, North Oxford and

standing base at Abingdon, and on 4 April Thomas Fairfax summoned Colonel Henry Ireton's dragoons and cavalry to join what was to be the last siege of Oxford. The first objective was to take control of all routes from the city, the London Road being the most important.

On 10 April the House of Commons demanded that all the King's garrisons in the stronghold should surrender, with harsh penalties if they refused. Underlying this demand was the now inevitable conclusion that, in Oxford at least, the Royalist cause was pretty much lost.

The Royalists refused to lie down, however. Troops clashed in Woodstock, and the noise of their cannon fire on 15 April could be heard in Oxford. The Parliamentarians, under Thomas Rainsborough, attacked the Royalist forces at Woodstock Manor House; but they were

DEADLY CHERWELL!

The Cherwell was a notorious source of accidents over the centuries:

- 🕱 'On Friday 6,' runs one typical press report from 1735, 'students belonging to Christ-church, Oxford, took a boat in order to fish the river Charrol [Cherwell] neer Islip, and by some accident the boat overset, whereby [one] was unfortunately drowned.'
- 🕱 Another, from August 1768, reports that the 'body of a poor servant girl of Oxford was found drowned in the Cherwell, opposite the Isle of Rhee, near which her hat had been found fastened to the grass. The cause of this poor creature's death is said to be owing to an Irish Journeyman Carpenter, who had kept company with her for some time, and under pretence of buying a Licence [to marry], &c. had defrauded her of what little money she had saved in service, as likewise part of her wearing apparel, and made off with them. The Coroner's Inquest brought in their verdict, Lunacy.'
- 🕱 In 1803, one Alice Bardgett was found drowned in a branch of the River Cherwell, near Christ Church Walk. 'It appeared … that the deceased had left her house for the purpose of searching for the body of Ann Cole, a young woman who had been missing several days; and it is supposed that the deceased, whilst looking for her, accidentally slipped into the said river.'
- 🕱 Another Oxford resident died whilst canoeing on the river in 1855, after bumping his friend's canoe for a 'lark': 'The stream was very rapid, and the bumped canoe went round with it several times, and in trying to right himself by some means the deceased lost his seat, the boat was consequently upset, and, melancholy to relate, he sank in something like sixteen feet of water, never to rise again alive…'
- 🕱 In 1894, 'The Hon. Mrs. Emily Margaret Feilding, daughter of the late Mr E.C. Egerton, M.P., has, we regret to state, been found drowned in the River Cherwell, at Oxford. The deceased lady, whose husband died only last year, had been missing since Monday morning last, when she announced her intention of taking a walk. On Friday some fear was enter-tained that she might have fallen into the river, and on the following afternoon the dragging operations revealed the lamentable truth.'
- 🕱 The famous boat race is not immune from disaster either: 'The Grade II listed boathouse of Oxford University Boat Club, home to Oxford crews competing in the Oxford and Cambridge Boat Race since 1881, was burnt to the ground during the night of 24 September [1999]. Arson is suspected… More than 40 rowing boats and many sets of oars were destroyed in the blaze and the replacement cost of this equipment alone is likely to be over £1 million. Also destroyed were historic records and photographs of Boat Race crews going back over 120 years.'

Marston, where a new bridge was built over the Cherwell.

Fairfax, after planning tactics with Oliver Cromwell (shortly to become Chancellor of the University) in Marston, arranged his army in a line from the Headington HQ, through St Clements and as far as Magdalen Bridge, just outside the city walls. The mustering besiegers were bombarded with cannon fire, and stones were hurled at them from the top of Magdalen bell tower. With the early wounded being stretchered off on either side, on 6 May Fairfax demanded that the defenders:

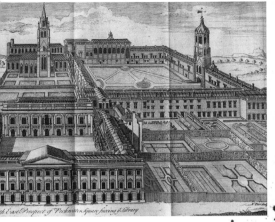

Above *Christ Church a century after the King's stay.*

Right *Christ Church Hall, home to Charles I's Parliament and the target of Fairfax's guns.*

...deliver up the City of Oxford into my hands, for the use of the Parliament. I very much desire the preservation of that place (so famous for learning), from ruin, which inevitably is like to fall upon it, except you concur. You may have honourable terms for yourself and all within that garrison if you reasonably accept thereof. I desire the answer this day.

Fairfax did not get the answer he had hoped for, and on 13 May he ordered his artillery to fire from Headington Hill, the first shower of shot falling in Christ Church Meadow. A further letter from Colonel Payne painted a brief summary of what followed, saying: 'There was a great meeting in Oxford, at which Sir Thomas got some blows among the rout, and narrowly escaped with his life'.

But in spite of this apparently reassuring show of Royalist defence, on 15 May King Charles' Privy Council in Oxford negotiated a ceasefire, and the house at Mill Lane was nominated as a meeting place for opposing generals to hammer out a treaty of surrender. The legality of the Privy Council's white-flag waving was immediately called into question by the officers of the garrison of Oxford, who thought they could win the war against Fairfax and Cromwell without premature treaties. The governor of the city, tail between his legs, had to advise the army that the King had confirmed the Privy Council to be his legal representative during his absence, and in this manner the will of the council was imposed on the very angry Royalist army, which openly declared that it had been betrayed by its own commanders. In a letter of formal

PASSING OUT

⟡

The men evacuated after the siege of Oxford had the following pass issued to them by the benevolent Thomas Fairfax:

> You are to suffer the Bearer — who was in the City and Garrison of Oxford at its Surrender, and is to have the full benefit of the Articles &c., quietly and without interruption to pass your Guards with his Servants, horses, arms, and goods and so repair to London or elsewhere upon his necessary occasions. And in all places where he shall reside or remove, he is to be protected from violence to his person, goods or estate according to these Articles, and to have full liberty within 6 months to go to any convenient port, and transport himself with his servants, goods and necessaries beyond the Seas, and in all other things to enjoy the benefit of the said Articles. Hereunto you are to give obedience, as you will answer the contrary.

OXFORD ISLAND

⟡

The Royalists had intended building elaborate defences around Oxford. According to plans drawn up by leading Dutch engineer of the age, Sir Bernard de Gomme, the entire city and suburbs were to be enclosed by banks, ditches and walls, shaped like a gigantic misshapen star. Each straight section of the starry walls would have been as long as Cornmarket; but the plan never got beyond the first few earthworks. Sir Bernard also planned to dam the rivers and flood the outskirts of Oxford, transforming it into an island (*see* p.44).

Work on de Gomme's schemes was slow. Charles enlisted townsfolk, but refused to pay them. As a result, of 122 pressganged navvies, only 12 turned up. University students, more pro-Royalist than the average townsman, did some of the work – it was noted by an observer that 'night and day [they] gall their hands with mattocks and shovels.'

The only remains of Civil War Royalist defence works are some earth banks between Merton and Balliol sports fields, and in gardens at Wadham College and Rhodes House. Parliamentarian lumps and bumps can be found in Marston, and in South Park.

⟡

complaint the officers of the army stated: 'that what inconvenience soever should arise to the King's Cause or his friends upon this Treaty is not in our hands to prevent'.

Amidst these rumblings of mutiny thirteen men from each side met in Mill Lane on 18 May. A war or words ensued, and it was not until 22 May that Fairfax was able to send a first draft of the Treaty of Surrender to the House of Commons. By 25 May this had been torn up, and in London a Committee of nine Royalists from the House of Lords and nine negotiators from the House of Commons agonised over further conditions for the surrender of Oxford. The key moment almost came when a letter from King Charles was produced – actually written back on the 18th from Newcastle upon Tyne:

> Trusty and well-beloved, we greet you well. Being desirous to stop the further effusion of the blood of our subjects, and yet respecting the faithful services of all in that City of Oxford which have faithfully served us and hazarded their lives for us:

we have thought it good to command you to quit that City, and disband the forces under your charge there, you receiving Honourable Conditions for you and them.

POSTAL STRIKE

However, many believed that Fairfax could force better terms with a military victory, and so the contents of this letter were not actually communicated to Oxford until 15 June. Battling on in ignorance of the King's effective surrender, and of the Commons' withheld information, Fairfax produced an amended treaty on 30 May for the surrender of the city, and the defending commissioners of the army bowed to it, saying that 'they submitted to the Fate of the Kingdom', even though they had faith in the 'strength of the tenableness of the Garrison'.

Underlining the latter point, they bombarded the Parliamentarian positions with cannon fire, and Fairfax's army retaliated in like manner. An estimated 200 cannon balls whizzed over enemy lines, one of them penetrating the Headington Hill ranks and killing the unfortunate Colonel Cotsworth.

For a while the embryonic peace treaty seemed nothing more than a piece of paper. Fairfax continued to harry the enemy, with a symbolic victory scored when Charles Fort, a key part of the city's defences, was captured by Colonel Weldon. Fairfax declared that he would still take Oxford by storm if necessary, aware that the enemy no longer commanded any of the exits from the city. On 3 June hungry Oxford horsemen, stomachs well and truly besieged, attempted to herd some Cowley cows into the city to supplement diminishing Royalist stores, but Parliamentarian horsemen met them with arms and beat them back.

For all his posturing, Fairfax was still concentrating on the treaty of surrender. By 10 June he was sufficiently confident of negotiations to send a fraternal gift to his enemy the Duke of York (the future James II), holed up in the city. This consisted of 'a Brace of Bucks, two muttons, two veals, two lambs, and six capons'. No Cowley cows, note.

With the war effectively over, and with Royalist soldiers mutineering and bringing some traditional wartime rape-and-pillage terror to the streets of Oxford, on 20 June the Articles of Surrender were finally signed, having been agreed by both sides at Water Eaton. The signing was carried out in the Audit House at Christ Church, the key signatories being the Governor of Oxford, and triumphant Thomas Fairfax.

On 22 June the fallen hero Prince Rupert and 300 Royalist aristocrats were given safe passage from the city, and two days later the treaty came into operation. Fairfax's army patrolled the streets to maintain order, and the Royalist evacuation began, with 3,000 soldiers marching from the city that had not succumbed, by military means, to three successive sieges.

OXFORD'S FIRST WHODUNNIT

JONATHAN BRADFORD DID not seem a man destined for a big footnote in posterity. He was described as bearing 'an unexceptional character', keeping a low profile as landlord of an inn on the London Road near Oxford. But notoriety came his way with the arrival of Christopher Hayes, riding to the city with his footman to see his relations in the year 1736.

Stopping for the night at Bradford's inn, Hayes shared his supper table with two other guests who occupied a room next to his, and, after a drink or two too many, he mentioned the large amount of money he was carrying about his person. The company retired to their respective beds, but the two supper guests had their slumber disturbed by a loud groaning from the adjoining room. The noise became increasingly distressing, and the men decided that Hayes must need assistance. Hurrying next door, they discovered a scene as red-handed as could be. Hayes was writhing on his bed in blood-soaked sheets, and poised over him with a knife in one hand and a lantern in the other was Jonathan Bradford.

The two men leapt upon the innkeeper, disarmed him and called him a murderer. Indeed, a guilty man had perhaps never been caught so obviously in mid-guilt. Bradford, however, denied murdering poor Hayes – who, by this point, had breathed and bled his last.

Proclaiming innocence after being apprehended at the bedside of a murdered man with a knife in your hand is always going to be a tricky corner to defend. But Bradford made a bold stab. According to a newspaper report: 'he assumed by this time an air of innocence, positively denied the crime, and asserted that he came there with the same humane intentions as themselves; for that, hearing a noise, he got out of bed, struck a light, armed himself with a knife for his defence, and had but that minute entered the room before them'.

Arrested and imprisoned in Oxford, Bradford maintained throughout that he was innocent. He protested this fact so often that an irritated justice retorted at one point: 'Mr Bradford, either you or myself committed this murder!' The case

Bradford discovers the corpse.

MARY BLANDY - GALLOWS CELEB

Mary Blandy of Henley, executed in 1752, was the most celebrated victim of the Oxford gallows, a fame which not even Jonathan Bradford and Giles Covington (*see* p.65) could eclipse.

The last woman to be executed in Oxford, and middle class too, she died – and murdered – for love. This was a winning combination for the public, and the case was elevated to national fame. Pamphlets and post-mortems were still being penned decades after the deed was done, some of the publications coming from Mary's own family, and containing all manner of apocryphal utterances from Ms Blandy.

Mary Blandy in irons.

Mary had fallen in love with William Henry Cranston, an army officer and son of a Scottish nobleman. Her fussy father did not approve of the match, and so Mary poisoned her parent with arsenic, claiming in court that she had intended the draft as a love potion to make him approve of the marriage. She was also accused of assisting the deaths of her mother and another relation.

Mary professed her innocence from the gallows, prayed for 15 minutes, and thanked the judges for their 'mild proceedings'. Then, according to a contemporary local report: 'She mounted the ladder with great cheerfulness, and a becoming decency, desired the prayers of all present, and having said a short prayer, she pulled the handkerchief over her eyes, and was turned off'. She was buried alongside her father in Henley-on-Thames.

came up at the next Assize court in Oxford, and Bradford pleaded not guilty. But he did not have much hope: the men who had discovered him claimed that he 'betrayed the signs of a guilty man' when they burst in on him, and the knife he held was covered in blood. The defence protested that Bradford's reactions and expression at the bedside 'were merely the terrors of humanity... on beholding such a horrid scene'. The jury, however, didn't even bother leaving the box before handing out a verdict of 'Guilty'.

Bradford's last words, before hanging on the city gallows, were predictable: 'I am innocent!' he cried, even as the noose was fitted.

Oxford Castle's prison tower.

'The world owes this knowledge to a remorse of conscience in the footman on a bed of sickness; it was a death-bed repentance, and by that death the law lost its victim!', says an account written in a Suffolk newspaper nearly seventy years after the event.

But the web tangled further when, after this revelation, the clergyman who had administered the last rights to Bradford made his own confession. The innkeeper was innocent of the crime, just as he had asserted throughout, but only because the footman got there first. Bradford had entered the chamber with the intention of murdering and robbing, and was flabbergasted to discover that someone had beaten him to it. He had turned back the sheets to examine the dying man, and dropped his knife in terror at what he saw. It was just after he had retrieved the now-bloody weapon that the neighbouring men burst onto the scene and manhandled him.

Eighteen months later, the footman who had accompanied Christopher Hayes to the London Road inn confessed. He had stabbed his employer, taken his money and gold watch and pocketed his silver snuff box, whose value was nothing to be sneezed at. After this, said the newspaper report, 'he escaped to his room', one of history's more gentle examples of fleeing from justice. Mere seconds afterwards, Bradford entered the scene.

ASSIZE ISN'T EVERYTHING

Serious criminal cases used to be judged at the periodic Courts of Assize (replaced, in 1972, by the Crown Court).

- Oxford was one of England's Assize Towns, providing lengthy, gory material for the local press. It was part of the 'Oxford Circuit', its roving court taking in many towns including Abingdon, Hereford, Worcester, Gloucester, Monmouth, Shrewsbury and Stafford.
- Minor cases were dealt with by other limbs of the law. Held four times a year, the regional Quarter Sessions sorted the criminal wheat from the chaff. Oxfordshire's were held in Oxford and Banbury.
- Minor offences were processed by Justices of the Peace at local Magistrates' Courts, or 'petty sessions'.
- In addition, the towns had various cells and dungeons, and larger villages had lock-ups for drunkards and other anti-socials. The windowless pyramidal folly near the children's playground in Wheatley, just beyond the eastern edge of Oxford, is a fine survival of the village lock-up.

RIOT AT THE KING'S HEAD TAVERN!

IN 1714 QUEEN Anne, last of the Stuart monarchs, died, and the Hanoverians, with non-English speaking George I, Anne's second cousin, came to the throne.

Oxford was not happy with this succession. The city had always favoured the Stuarts, combining this with a staunch support of the Church of England. (James II caused a minor uprising when he installed a Catholic head at Magdalen College in 1687, though University College still saw fit to erect a statue of him a little later). When, in the 1690s, a group of Jacobite ringleaders – rebels supporting the return of the deposed James and his heirs – were acquitted, Oxford undergraduates took to the streets in celebration. They also marked the death of Queen Mary with concealed joy, sensing that the royal line would have to veer back to James and his son James (soon to be styled 'The Old Pretender').

Oxford was not among the many towns that staged 'coronation riots' when George I was crowned. But there was still a simmering disapproval from Town and Gown alike as the official town celebrations took place, and the new King was widely ridiculed. A brief summary of his personal attributes was scrawled on a College wall, declaring 'A KING, A CUCKOLD, A PRINCE, A BASTARD'.

The simmer only began to boil over when the Old Pretender wrote to the University in 1715, claiming that the new Hanoverian

George I, whose coronation sparked riots.

establishment planned to undermine its powers and seize University land. When the city officially celebrated George I's birthday on 28 May that year, the first riots erupted. Malcontents, numbering thousands according to some pro-Jacobite reports, converged outside The King's Head tavern on the High Street, favourite watering hole of pro-establishment Whigs. Stones were thrown, one man receiving a deep head wound, and the town's celebratory Georgian bonfire was dismantled, opportunistic protesters smuggling away most of the faggots for their own hearths. At the height of the protest the chant 'Murder them!' passed ominously through the throng.

High Street, Oxford, in the Georgian era. The King's Head Tavern was located here.

The mob was soon reinforced by drinkers from neighbouring pubs, and the Whigs had to flee through a back entrance. Proctors from the Colleges (the University police) managed to restore some degree of order, but the whole thing flared up again later when a Whig from Oriel College, bastion of Establishment support, fired his gun and injured a Brasenose student. Any window sporting a candle – a mark of loyal celebration of the King's birthday – was pelted with stones. Turning their attentions from the successfully holed-up Whigs, the rioters then attacked a Presbyterian meeting house in St Ebbes, doing a great deal of damage and using the makeshift chapel's furniture to construct their own bonfire, mocking the official fires of the birthday celebrations.

Presbyterian minister William Roby, staunch supporter of the Hanoverian succession, was put in the town stocks, according to some accounts. His effigy was burnt too, Guy Fawkes-like. Town constables were too few in number to disperse the crowds, and could only look on, or hide.

Things were even more fevered on the following day, 29 May, anniversary of the Restoration of Stuart King Charles II. It was very unfortunate timing, having George's birthday back-to-back with this auspicious date. Oxford celebrated as if the Restoration was happening all over again, students wearing sprigs of oak in their hats and lighting bonfires, to such an extent that authorities feared the city might be burnt down. People ran through the streets shouting 'King James III! The true King! No usurper!' Oriel College was stoned and several people were injured. Dissenting chapels were attacked – a popular target for pro-Church of England protesters – and some Baptist and Presbyterian meeting places were demolished in the frenzy.

Impressive as this initial outburst had been, the riots faded away in Oxford, and although there was widespread backing for the Old Pretender's attempts to invade and reconquer, the city lacked the will to join the organised national revolt. The clergy's official line was to condemn the Jacobites, and in spite of strong support for the revolt in 1715 and an unofficial stocktaking of the available men, horses and arms that could support the rebel Duke of Ormond (who was expected to lead the Jacobite cause in the south), order was maintained. It's true that mobs gathered, Riot Acts were read, buildings were destroyed, and on-the-street face-offs with swords and pistols took place, but majority loyalty won the day.

Fears of a Jacobite takeover of Oxford lingered for many months, however. A consignment of smuggled arms – 140 swords and 244 bayonets – was intercepted in October 1715, and dragoons made a lightning raid a little later to arrest suspected ringleaders. The mayor spoke of 'pestilent fellows who fomented sedition', even as open chants supporting 'James III' and Ormond were heard from gangs promenading the streets. But the feared rebellion effectively came to an end when three chief Oxford conspirators, Gordon, Kerr and Dorwell, were sentenced to death and hanged at Tyburn in London on 7 December 1715. New bouts of pro-Jacobite violence coloured the first half of 1716, but failed to rekindle the requisite level of support. Thirty years passed, the Old Pretender died – but the story was far from over.

The hysteria and speculation surrounding the Jacobite invasion of 1745 was to simmer for many years. The rebellion of 'Young Pretender' Charles Edward Stuart, grandson of James II, made it as far south as Derby in that year, before retreating back to Scotland where the uprising met its nemesis at the Battle of Culloden in April 1746. But there were still many citizens in England who wanted to remove the incumbent Hanoverian Georges from the throne, and Oxford folklore maintains that two Jacobite students were hanged under Magdalen Bridge in 1745 for belonging to the pro-Pretender White Rose Club.

- George I was Queen Anne's second cousin - there were over fifty surviving Stuart heirs with closer blood claims to the throne.
- The direct line of the royal House of Stuart flickered out with the death of Cardinal Henry Benedict Stuart, brother of Charles Edward, in 1807. But there are still heirs via indirect descent, the current one being Duke Francis of Bavaria.
- Fascinatingly, if Queen Elizabeth II's grandson Prince William becomes King he will be the first British monarch descended from James I since Queen Anne. His mother, Diana, Princess of Wales, was descended from the lines of both Charles II and James II.

Charles II, from whose line Diana was descended, as a young boy. (With kind permission of the Thomas Fisher Rare Book Library, University of Toronto)

Evelyn Waugh, a member of the White Rose Club. (Library of Congress, Prints & Photographs Division, Carl Van Vechten Collection, LC-USZ62-42514)

University students enthusiastically debated the Jacobite versus Hanoverian question in the light of the Young Pretender, and some decided to turn all the hot air into action. In February 1748 they took to the streets again; by now Jacobite feeling had become an underground rumbling in the city rather than a willingness to jump to arms. However, the University Vice Chancellor, Proctors and Heads still feared that things were careering towards outright insurrection, and in April they formally condemned the students involved, making 'a public declaration of our sincere abhorrence and detestation of such factions and seditious practices, as also of our firm resolution to punish offenders (of what state or quality soever they are) who shall duly be convicted thereof, according to the uttermost severity and rigour of our statutes'. The 'soever they are' note was a warning that offenders would not be able to hide behind titles and peerages.

Several of the ringleaders – 'beardless striplings of sedition', according to the summary in the *Newgate Calendar*, one of the most popular publications of the nineteenth century – were apprehended. Two students, John Whitmore and Jeremiah Dawes, were found guilty and were fined, imprisoned for two years, and told to find two 'sureties' who would be personally responsible for their behaviour over the following seven years. They were also commanded 'that they immediately walk round Westminster Hall, with a label affixed to their foreheads, denoting their crime and sentence... They accordingly were each labelled on the forehead and led round the Hall, stopping at each Court to solicit pardon, and then sent to prison.' This public-school style ritual humiliation was reserved for cases of sedition, it seems.

The year 1748 was to be the last year of noteworthy Jacobitism in Oxford. The town had now entrenched its loyalist position, and any lingering support for the cause was reduced to a philosophical and sentimental level, the lingering expression of which was the University's officially outlawed (and therefore highly attractive) White Rose Club. New member Evelyn Waugh wrote in 1923: 'I also joined the White Rose Club, an occasional dining club devoted to the Stuart cause ...'

1 VIEW OF OXFORD. (LC-DIG-PPMSC-08764)

The 'dreaming spires' belie the city's dark and gruesome underbelly. Behind the academic veneer is a tale of Saxon versus Dane ethnic cleansing, 'Town versus Gown' riots, public executions and civil wars.

Opposite 2 MAGDALEN FOUNDER'S TOWER AND CLOISTERS. (LC-DIG-PPMSC-08768)

The Founder in question was Lord Chancellor William Waynflete, who in 1458 turfed out the sick and needy from the Hospital of St. John, earmarking the site for a new college. The building work took 50 years to complete. James II caused a minor uprising when he installed a Catholic head here in 1687.

Background 3 MAGDALEN FROM THE RIVER.(LC-DIG-PPMSC-08767)

In 1646 Roundhead General Fairfax camped out by the river near Magdalen. Royalists holed up in the College catapulted stones at his army. The anti-Stuart lobby got its revenge in 1745 when two Jacobite students were hanged under Magdalen Bridge.

Above 4 MAGDALEN TOWER. (LC-DIG-PPMSC-08769)

Also known as the Main Tower, or Bell Tower, from which vantage point King Charles I watched his cannons fire at the New Model Army in 1644. Carol singing occurs here every 1 May, harking back to 1509 when a requiem was sung from the top of the newly completed tower to mark the death of Henry VII, who had died a few weeks earlier.

Opposite above 5 MERTON COLLEGE. (LC-DIG-PPMSC-08766)

Students were forced to hide here to avoid being scalped by an angry mob in 1355. Later, it was the site of Civil War earthworks, built in preparation for the Siege of Oxford.

Opposite below 6 NEW COLLEGE FRONT GARDEN. (LC-DIG-PPMSC-08771)

Founded on a rubbish dump and plague pit in the fourteenth century, New College was used as an arms depot during the Civil War. During World War I its grounds were filled with hospital tents to shelter victims of the battlefield.

7 THE SHELDONIAN. (LC-DIG-PPMSC-08775)

Designed by Christopher Wren, the Theatre was completed in 1668. The 13 stone heads that surround the building are known as The Emperors. The current ones, dating from the early 1970s, are the third generation. The first set was ousted in 1868, but their replacements were defaced by undergraduates (and damaged by the scouring that sought to remedy the vandalism). John Betjemen described them in 1925 as "mouldering busts".

8 ST JOHN'S, BUILT ON THE BONES OF THE ST BRICE'S DAY MASSACRE. (LC-DIG-PPMSC-08772).

Slaughtered during Anglo-Saxon ethnic cleansing in 1002AD, the remains of the murdered Danes were not discovered until 2010.

9 TOM TOWER. (LC-DIG-PPMSC-08776

Designed by Christopher Wren and built in 1682, the tower houses Old Tom. This is one of the original bells of the twelfth century Osney Abbey, and was originally called 'Mary'. It was recast for Tom Tower, and rehung in 1953. It is Oxford's loudest bell, and chimes 101 times at five past nine every night.

10 TRINITY. (LC-DIG-PPMSC-08773)

In 1883 Frederick Burnard, a coachman at Trinity College, became the first fatality of St Giles Fair when he fell from a roundabout and fractured his skull.

11 CHRIST CHURCH COLLEGE. (LC-DIG-PPMSC-08765)

Its walls were targeted by Roundhead cannons during the Civil War. But it also ushered in peace – the Articles of Surrender were signed here in 1646.

CONDEMNED TO HANG – FOREVER!

ON **21 MAY** 1790 in Reading, Richard Kilby was flogged after deserting the Berkshire Regiment, at a time when military conscription wasn't the sort of thing you could argue with. But Kirby wasn't too worried about the ordeal, knowing that far weightier matters were about to engulf him.

On the following day Kilby was questioned about a robbery at Abingdon, along with other criminal charges, and under interrogation he confessed to a crime that wasn't even on the magistrate's list of allegations. On the evening of Michaelmas Fair in Abingdon, September 1787, he had met with accomplices Giles Covington, Charles Shury and John Castle, and mugged a Scotsman called David Charteris who was going home to Toot Baldon after a day at the fair. The victim was robbed of 40 guineas and bludgeoned to death. The murder took place at Nuneham Courtenay, near Oxford.

Shury was captured, and he and Kilby were removed to the prison at Oxford Castle. A couple of days later John Castle, captured at Sparsholt, joined them. This just left Giles Covington, and a large bounty (70 guineas) was placed on his head to encourage his swift apprehension. Castle and Shury were condemned to the gallows, and executed in the summer of 1790, their bodies afterwards sent to surgeons at Christ Church to be 'anatomised' – i.e. used for dissection and lectures. Kilby, who had 'squealed', avoided the tryst with the hangman as reward for his information.

The confession of a recently executed criminal nicknamed Oxford Tom had implicated Covington in yet another capital offence, the murder of a woman who had been robbed and thrown off Culham Bridge. Quite how much he knew of all these accusations and revelations is unknown, as he was serving in the navy at

DISSECT DUMAS

One typical example of anatomisation was highwayman 'Darkin, alias Dumas,' executed in Oxford in 1761 for highway robbery. 'His behaviour was extremely undaunted; for when he came out of the gaol to the ladder, he ascended it with the greatest resolution... he put the cord round his own neck... pulled out a white handkerchief, tied it round his eyes and face, and went off without saying a word.

'His body was ordered to be brought back into the castle, to be conveyed to the Museum for dissection; but he declaring that he valued not death, but only the thoughts of being anatomized, a large gang of bargemen arose, took him away in triumph, carried him to the next parish church; and while some rung bells for joy, others opened his belly, filled it with unslack'd lime, and then buried the body.'

the time... However, all seamen return to port at some point.

HELLO SAILOR...

On 5 March 1791, London's *Evening Post* was pleased to announce:

> On Monday last, Giles Freeman Covington, one of the accomplices in the inhuman murder of David Charteris in September 1786, near Nuneham Wood (in company with Shury and Castle, who were executed at this place last Summer Assize), was brought here by two of the officers from Bow Street. The apprehending this most atrocious offender has been attended with circumstances which appear highly providential.

Covington was swiftly tried and condemned on 4 March, the newspaper report noting that the 'pathetic and animated speech' of the judge 'appeared to have far greater effect upon the court than the prisoner'. Giles appears to have been far more angry with Kilby than anyone else during the proceedings. The latter, as part of the deal to save his own neck, had given evidence

against his former companion; and, choosing his moment, Covington broke away from his guards and leapt at Kilby, taking a swing at his head before being dragged back to his position in the dock.

It was Covington's last act of defiance. Led from the court, he was soon contemplating the prospect of death and damnation. And then he remembered a very important detail in this unfortunate affair: he was innocent.

BYE BYE SAILOR...

Well, that's what Covington now insisted. He impressed the prison chaplain with his words of repentance and the zeal with which he addressed his prayers. More to the point, he wanted to make a statement setting out proof of his own innocence in the murder of David Charteris. He admitted that he had committed crimes in his life, but he had not been with Kilby and the others on the day of the murder.

A letter was duly written, but fell on deaf ears; and, still proclaiming his innocence, Giles had to reconcile himself to the gallows. A large crowd turned out on 7 March 1791 at Oxford Castle to see him die. Before he took the plunge, Covington, decked out in his sailor's uniform complete with white gloves and white hatband, tossed a letter in the air, asking that it should be read out. But without hanging around to see his request carried out, he jumped to his death.

The letter was a brave and well-constructed letter from a man who was scarcely literate. It must have been composed with the assistance of the chaplain, or perhaps a literate fellow prisoner. Addressed to magistrate Christopher Willoughby, it included the melodramatic plea: 'I hope you and your family will live to find that Giles Freeman Covington died innocent and then I hope you would relieve the widow that is left behind if Bedlam is not to be her doom', Bedlam being London's infamous lunatic asylum.

Covington's body was cut down and delivered to Dr Pegge at Christ Church for the Anatomy School. Giles was carved up as the main course at the following day's public lecture. When there was nothing more to be carved, the bones were wired together, and the skeleton of Giles Covington became a teaching aid.

In 1860 the bones were displayed in the new University Museum of Natural

DISSECTION - A NO-BRAINER

Giles was not alone in being picked to pieces after death. Prior to the Anatomy Act of 1832 it was common practice for judges to condemn victims to the gallows first and the dissection table afterwards. In 2000 an archaeological dig at the Old Ashmolean (the Museum of the History of Science) shed a little light on what was being handed over to the nineteenth-century professors of anatomy at the University.

☠ In all, 2,050 human bones were unearthed during the dig, belonging to between fifteen and thirty individuals buried during the seventeenth and eighteenth centuries. They were mainly adult males – not surprising given the usual victims of the gallows – but also included three foetuses, an adolescent boy and two women. The skulls of the adults had been sawn in half, indicating that the brain had been removed for pickling.

☠ In addition there were 900 animal bones, the most unusual being the fore-limb of a manatee - the animal sometimes mistaken for a mermaid by short-sighted sailors, according to folklore.

Old Ashmolean.

THE RESURRECTION OF ANN GREEN

The biggest celebrity of the dissection table was Ann Green. Hanged in 1650 in Oxford's cattle yard for the murder of her newborn child, her death had been assisted by spectators who swung from her legs so boisterously that they had to be dispersed, out of fear that the gallows would break.

After half an hour Ann was officially declared dead, cut down and carted to Christ Church Anatomy School to colour the afternoon lecture. Three doctors gathered, scalpels poised – at which point she gasped for air, and the would-be dissectors spent the next few hours employing resuscitation, hot drinks, blood-letting, massage, hot bandages, warm beds and compression of the arms and legs to fully revive her.

After twelve hours Ann spoke, and over the next few days she regained her memory; her swollen face returned to normal and her motor functions were slowly restored. News of the recovery spread and, accepting it all as a weird miracle, the Oxford justices reprieved the poor woman.

Anne Green later married and had three children, keeping her coffin as a macabre souvenir, and surviving her own execution by fifteen years.

These days, death and disaster are followed by a rash of poor-taste jokes. It was no different back then. Hot on the heels of the amazing story came the anonymous:

Ann Green was a slippery quean,
In vain did the jury detect her;
She cheated Jack Ketch, and then the vile wretch
'Scap'd the knife of the learned Dissector.

History on Parks Road. It stood here in its glass case well into the 1960s, with a label which deserves a nomination for Most Useless Museum Label Ever. It read simply 'Englishman'.

Tossed into the rubbish tip known as the Bone Room, it was only the subtle inscription 'Giles Covington' on the lower jaw bone that saved it. A member of staff did a little research and unearthed the whole sorry tale, and the remains were offered to the Museum of Oxford. And, in spite of ongoing attempts to have the bones buried, and to have the man's name cleared by Royal Pardon, Giles is still hanging there.

Skeleton of Giles Covington.

DEATH IN VICTORIAN OXFORD!

CHOLERA WAS ONE of the principle killers in Europe during the nineteenth century, wiping out tens of millions worldwide. Associated with unsanitary conditions, and transmitted largely through contaminated water, it often devastated entire cities. Oxford certainly didn't escape, three major outbreaks laying people low in 1832, 1849, and 1854.

Early analyses pinpointed unwholesome air as the cause of the disease, and the foul odours were indeed indicative of the real menace: filthy water laden with infected faeces. Cholera is an intestinal infection caused by the malignant bacterium *Vibrio cholerae*. Diarrhoea and vomiting are its main symptoms, and the process of transmission becomes almost unstoppable once the bacterium has contaminated the water supply. The diarrhoea is horrifically severe – up to 20 litres a day in acute cases – and leads to rapid dehydration and, without rehydration, death.

Amongst the less uplifting of his *Recollections of Oxford* (1868), writer G.V. Cox reports on the city's outbreaks in grisly detail:

1832: Oxford, in this July, was visited with many cases of cholera, including forty deaths. A great cry was raised against that filthy stream, which empties itself into the Isis at Folly Bridge, and

whose banks were lined with 'pigsties and other abominations'. The Christ Church authorities, however, succeeded in making the stream partially cleanse itself, by a system of flashes of water, and at a very great expense shut it out, at least from the eye, by carrying a wall along its course on the west of Christ Church Meadow. Strict rules were enforced, pigsties were relegated to the suburbs, and a standing Board of Health kept a watchful look-out. St. Clement's also has its dirty stream, and the greatest number of cases (and fatal ones) occurred there, especially at the house of the Common-room man at Magdalen College – not indeed by the river-side but on Cowley Road, and belonging to a very

Folly Bridge.

1854: Sept. 7. The dreaded cholera again showed itself in Oxford, and continued to carry off its victims through the month, though in small numbers compared with the former visitation. Happily, it disappeared as October commenced; but it was thought safer by the authorities to call up the Undergraduates a week later than usual.

DEATH BY PRIVY!

In August 1839, 'at the Town Hall tavern', an inquest was made on 'the body of Amelia Ovenell, aged two years, daughter of Mr. Ovenell, boot and shoe maker, of St. Aldate's parish, [who] was suffocated by falling into a privy.

'Mr. Hall, the landlord of the Town Hall tavern, and Mrs. Knibbs, a neighbour, succeeded in getting the child out of the privy, and Mr. Robert Stone, surgeon, of this city... endeavoured to restore animation, but without success. Verdict, accidentally suffocated.'

During the 1832 outbreak an estimated 1 per cent of the Oxford population caught the disease. W.P. Ormerod, surgeon at the Radcliffe Infirmary, wrote a report on the epidemic in 1848, titled (and misspelt) *On the Sanatory Condition of Oxford*. He predicted that another outbreak would soon occur – that was, indeed, the main reason behind his publication, to warn the city that complacency would breed disaster. Cholera was, he said, 'advancing towards us on its old track, and with similar characters'. The following year his fears were borne out.

The epidemic of 1832 had spread through the country with alarming speed, devastating the land and then moving on, like a plague of invisible locusts:

respectable family. The cholera carried off Mrs. G–, two grown-up daughters, and a maid-servant. Of the total number of deaths in July and August (viz. forty), twenty-nine occurred in St. Clement's... It is very remarkable (we may well call it providential) that the cholera on its two appearances in Oxford broke out at the commencement of the Long-Vacation, and happily went down as the young men were beginning to come up for the Michaelmas Term.

1849: August. Cases of cholera were reported as spreading in Oxford; great care was taken by the Board of Health to check it... Oct. 6. The disease began to relax; there had, however, been 121 cases and 64 deaths. About the middle of October it was publicly announced that the cholera had entirely disappeared in Oxford. Deo gratias! In 1849 St Sepulchre's Cemetery in Jericho opened, as an overflow for existing graveyards choked with cholera victims.

The cholera appeared in England on Oct. 26, 1831, and reached Oxford in about eight months, on June 24, 1832. The last case of cholera occurred in Oxford Nov. 28, 1832, and the last case in England on December 31 of the same year. The disease prevailed here chiefly during the months of July, August, and September, the same period in which England suffered most. The number of cases in Oxford and St. Clement's, without St. Giles', amounted to one hundred and seventy-four, of which eighty-six died, and eighty-eight recovered...

The cholera appears to have affected the great part of Oxford more or less, St. Michael's, St. Mary the Virgin, and St. John's being the only parishes in which

CESS AND THE CITY!

Ormerod's contemporary descriptions of the city are chilling:

The large open drains of Oxford consist of two classes, those not communicating with any great source of water, and those forming branches of the river. To the former class belong the open drains of Jericho and Church Street St. Thomas': drains full of decomposing matters, with sluggish streams of the foulest kind, and running through parts which suffer severely from disease. To the second class belong the open streams of St. Thomas', St. Ebbe's, and St. Aldate's, which at times are full of water, whilst at other times they hardly flow at all; into these streams a great number of small drains open, and the exposure of the water amongst the houses to the open air appears to be connected with the high mortality from contagious diseases in their neighbourhood...

...A large number of courts are situated close to these open drains, and in some cases the houses extend partly over them, an entire court or a single house being thus exposed to the most unwholesome nuisance... Cesspools are exceedingly common, and independently of their unhealthiness under all circumstances in the immediate neighbourhood of houses, there are serious inconveniences from their not being attended to. Thus in one instance the drain-water at times floods the court, and not unfrequently the odours pass up into the confined courts from the imperfection of the drain. In one place there is a kind of small cesspool in the course of a drain, immediately in front of a house-door, only covered by a wooden door: and in another there is a cesspool forming an open pond at the end of a court...

In a large number of courts the drain is insufficiently guarded to prevent smells passing up, or so choked up at times as to prevent things passing down. In one case, the house where fatal fever existed was just opposite a drain of this kind... The court, and even the house, appears to be flooded in some cases with foul water from this cause. At times also a drain passes under a cottage floor or a house cellar, and renders parts of the house almost unbearable...

Many of the courts are narrow, confined, and hardly admit fresh air; and in others the floor, from being earthen, or full of holes, is soaked with drain water; in such cases the inhabitants cannot get rid of the refuse, are exposed to the most unwholesome smells, and almost destitute of fresh air... There is great want in most courts of some place to put ashes and solid refuse in: these matters scattered about the court decompose and putrefy, as well as stop up the drain...

[The poor] themselves almost apologize for living in such places, or for not removing when their children die of fever, alleging their want of means to move or take any dwelling bearing a higher price.

Ormerod's report also points the finger at dirty lodging houses, said to 'receive any body, and the persons so admitted often violate all rules of decency in not availing themselves of the ordinary means of convenience'. Filthy dog kennels were also blamed, along with festering bone-yards such as the one blighting the parish of St Thomas (the bones being converted into fertiliser). Other hazards included pigsties, cowsheds, slaughterhouses, and dung heaps. The worst of the latter is described as 'a large manure-depot, consisting of heaps of refuse of great size and of the foulest kind'.

NOXIOUS RADCLIFFE

The institution that Ormerod worked for, the Radcliffe Infirmary, was not exactly a breath of fresh air itself. In 1784, philanthropist John Howard had given a bleak assessment of conditions there:

> The stories are too low; the height of the loftiest ward not being above 15 feet. From this fault, and the closeness of the windows, which I always found shut, the wards, especially the men's, are offensive beyond conception. The sewers are not sufficiently attended to, the beds improperly have testers and the kitchen is not well placed. The fanlights over the doors of the wards, in this, as in many other hospitals, are glazed. Were they open, it would tend to purify the air; or, at least, the noxious effluvia would become so sensible through the rest of the house, as might induce the matron, and the gentlemen who only attend in the committee room, to insist upon effectual means being used for a proper ventilation of the wards.

John Radcliffe, founder of public hospitals in Oxford, was renowned for his plain speaking. He once announced to the ailing, ulcerated William II that 'I would not have Your Majesty's two legs for your three kingdoms'. When another patient offered a paltry fee for the good doctor's attentions, Radcliffe repaid him by predicting his imminent death. The poor man died soon afterwards – out of terror, it is said.

Opened in 1770, the infirmary was the world's first hospital founded as a charity for people who could not afford to pay for treatment. The original institution excluded children, pregnant women and people with infectious diseases, although later benefactors plugged most of these gaps. The infirmary closed in 2007, and in 2012 it began a new life as University academic offices at the heart of the Radcliffe Observatory Quarter – the biggest building and redevelopment project in Oxford since the nineteenth century.

Radcliffe Infirmary in the early Victorian era.

it did not occur. The stress of the disease fell however on St. Clement's, St. Ebbe's, and St. Thomas' – i.e. the poorest areas of the city, where there were one hundred and forty-four cases... thirty-one in St. Ebbe's, forty in St. Thomas's, and seventy-three or more than the number in these two parishes together in St. Clement's alone.

Oxford's last outbreak was long ago; but worldwide cholera still causes more than 100,000 deaths a year, and incapacitates millions in the process.

DEATH BY BATH!

'[In June 1852], the public baths and wash-houses at Oxford were opened, and immediately afterwards the hot and cold water cisterns fell, bringing with them the tall shaft and walls adjoining. A boy named Burchell lost his life; the stoker, Wordsworth, was so severely injured that it is feared he cannot recover; his wife, who was with him, partaking of dinner, was very much bruised; a boy named Hosier had his thigh broken; and two little girls sustained considerable injury.' (*Liverpool Mercury*)

AD 1867

DEATH TO MAYOR GRUBB!

ON 15 NOVEMBER 1867, *The Daily Telegraph* waxed purple:

> Oxford in tumult and riotous confusion! Her stately streets crowded with angry and starving people, her Colleges shut up, and two companies of Grenadier Guards, with forty pounds of ammunition per man, bivouacked in her Corn Exchange! Such a spectacle has scarcely been witnessed since the days when Rupert's Cavaliers clattered through The High.

This tumult and riotous confusion all began with Alderman Isaac Grubb. He was Mayor of Oxford in 1857-8, and liked to think of himself as being at the forefront of social and political reform. A champion of 'Town' on the ancient 'Town versus Gown' axis of City and University, he was the man who in 1857 put an end to the annual public sermon and fine of St Scholastica's Day, 10 February, which since the days of the murderous riots of 1355 had seen mayors and other town officials do public penance for the Town's part in the slaughter of the Gown on that day.

Grubb's main business was bread, a fact that would lead him to his starring role in the Oxford Bread Riots of 1867. He had shops in St Clements, St Ebbes, St Michael's and St Peter-le-Bailey parishes. He was proud of his contribution in providing the ordinary working man

with the basics of sustenance, and did not lose the opportunity to promote the fact. In 1851 he took out an advert in *Jackson's Oxford Journal*:

> After another abundant harvest, gathered in in splendid order, it is nothing but fair and right that the public should reap the advantage... I. GRUBB takes this opportunity of returning his sincere thanks for the extensive support he has so long been honoured with, and trusts that he shall continue, for many years to

Bread riots in action!

come, to supply his friends and customers with GOOD AND CHEAP BREAD. The consumption of Oxford is about 700 sacks of flour a week, and if only half this quantity has been sold a penny a loaf cheaper... the Oxford public will have saved £20 a day, or £7,000 a year in this necessary article of food alone... the whole of which enormous sum the consumers of bread have been spared the spending, through the indomitable perseverance of one individual only, and that during the last 16 years. FACTS ARE STUBBORN THINGS.

EARNING A CRUST

Facts are, indeed, stubborn. When it became a known fact that Grubb had started selling his bread to the University at prices lower than those offered to the townsfolk (7.5 pence as opposed to 9 pence for a large loaf), his premises on Cornmarket became the focus of Bread Riots.

The University was a privileged island set apart from the rest of the city, which in the nineteenth century was seeing rising levels and poverty. The squalor of the St Ebbes Ward (long since burnt down and/or demolished and covered with such modern delights as the Westgate Shopping Centre) was on a par with the more notorious regions of the industrial North and Midlands, and many people here were unemployed.

Hope had raised its head in 1865 when the Great Western Railway planned to build its workshops in Oxford, promising more than 1,500 new jobs. But the University opposed the scheme, feeling that such industrial development would alter the character of the city. The poorer elements of the populace clearly played no part in their conception of this inherent 'character'. In consequence, the GWR built workshops in Swindon instead, much to

Old mansion in Cornmarket Street.

the fury of the 1,500 Oxford men denied those jobs. (The University was also to veto development of electric trams and an underground train line in the 1900s. Even a motorised bus service in 1913 was refused a licence.)

It didn't take much to stir the mob into action. Ironically it was radical champion of the people Isaac Grubb who bore the brunt of their anger. In November 1867, when it was revealed that the baker was supplying the Colleges, the mob, chanting 'Cheap bread!', decided to make him the toast of the town. *Jackson's Oxford Journal* reported:

An immense crowd, numbering about 600 or 800 men and boys, with a sprinkling of women, rushed along Cornmarket Street to the shop of Alderman Grubb, baker, amidst hooting and yelling and cries of 'We'll have our rights', 'We want cheap bread', etc.

GRUBB'S UP

Mayor Isaac Grubb had clashed with the city on numerous occasions.

- He refused to pay the tax to the Lamp Company, levied on businesses for their use of city-supplied gas light. Grubb's properties, the man argued, were not lit, and should therefore be exempt from the levy. He lost his case at formal hearings for two years running.
- He refused to attend Queen Victoria in formal court dress as Mayor because he had no wish 'to make a Tomfool of myself'.
- He refused to have 'that bauble' (the mayoral mace) present during official proceedings.
- He put a stop to the city's annual contribution to St Martin's church at Carfax, saying that such payments were not in step with the progressive measures of the 1835 Municipal Reform Act. When asked by the taxed populace where the council's money was being spent, Grubb was not going to reply, 'On an ancient tithe to the church'.
- None of which came as a surprise to the Conservative *Jackson's Oxford Journal* which, prior to the mayoral elections, had noted that the Liberal Isaac Grubb was 'of radical notoriety… his starting is looked on quite as a joke and has caused considerable merriment in the Ward'.

The 'bauble' so despised by Grubb.

St Martin's, Carfax.

The shop was, of course, closed; but the upper windows were speedily riddled with stones and threats of firing his premises were made.

Riotous University students, sensing a robust resurrection of Town versus Gown, had gathered to do battle with their old adversaries but were ordered back to their Colleges by the University Proctors. Those who ignored orders were later 'rusticated' (expelled from the University).

The Bread Rioters smashed windows in Grubb's Cornmarket and Queen Street outlets, and in his Summertown home too, before being scattered by the combined city and University authorities, twenty or so being arrested. Various bits of the mob then turned to the Colleges, putting rocks through windows and baying for blood. Satirical pamphlets were churned out, lampooning Mayor Carr (for his 'Mis-Carr-iage of justice', as they angrily punned) and the 'Maggotty gentleman' Grubb; and many men went on strike in support of the uprising.

A militia was called in – partly financed by none other than Isaac Grubb – comprising special constables and mounted Grenadier Guards from Windsor supplemented by special officers sourced locally. Magistrates issued an order for all boys to be kept indoors after 5 p.m. during the following week to avoid trouble. Students were told not to venture into Oxford after dark, pubs and shops were closed, and all musical bands and other means of drawing a crowd were banned. Even the scheduled performance in the Town Hall of *Jacob the Wizard* was cancelled. All grain stored in the town was removed by train for fear of theft.

On the 12th a crowd of thousands tramped through the streets, converging on Cornmarket to face off the makeshift army, whose numbers totalled less than 200. More windows were put through, including the police station's, but the Mayor, although he read the Riot Act, did not unleash his militia.

The angry mob mugged more students and smashed lots of windows during this restless month, outnumbering the hastily reinforced militia, and surging through the city streets a couple of thousand strong at the height of the protest. But alleged ringleaders were brought to trial and variously fined, imprisoned or sent for hard labour. The town corporation eventually capitulated and told all Oxford bakers – Grubb included – to slice one penny off the price of a loaf.

Of course, the rioters had not taken to the streets merely for the sake of bread prices and Isaac Grubb's double-dealing. Sandwiched between these complaints were the fundamental issues of poverty and unemployment. But the price reduction made the cause go stale, and by the end of the year the riots were over.

DEATH AND DISORDER AT ST GILES' FAIR

ST GILES' FAIR, which takes over the wide thoroughfare of St Giles every year in early September, has survived for 300 or 400 years (its exact origins being obscure), in spite of various attempts to suppress it. It is one of the largest street fairs of its kind anywhere in the world and if each year a theft, fight or accident makes the local headlines, it is certainly nothing new.

On the surface St Giles' has always been a good-humoured showcase of gaudy and low-brow entertainment, from the latest Victorian swingboat rides to the newest stomach-churning scream-alongs. But this 'pleasure fair' character of the event is relatively new – the fair existed for a few centuries without the swings and roundabouts, as a collection of trading stalls, travelling exhibitions and theatrical events. These ranged from pricey mobile zoos and circuses to the low budget delights of performances such as the one advertised in 1819 with: 'Monsieur Louis Colombier', who 'Will Dance A Hornpipe Blindfolded, Amongst Nine Real Eggs'.

But beneath the fun and games, opportunistic violence and accident were never far from the surface. The following is a selection of incidents as reported in *Jackson's Oxford Journal* over the years.

1827: William Williams, 'dealer in spiced nuts etc.,' was on his way to St Giles' Fair to sell his wares when he was accosted by two men, both wearing paper tucked under their hats to conceal their faces. Taking note of his stock of 'gingerbread nuts' they declared 'if you have goods to sell, you have money to give away: we want money, and money we must have before we leave you, if not, we will knock you down with this stick.' Flourishing a bludgeon over Williams' head, one of the men said, 'Let us have your money and your bundle, and we won't ill-use you; we know you very well, and when we are better off, we will return it to you again.'

They then robbed him of 13s 6d, nicked his nuts and other goods, and threatened to murder him if he watched their retreat or mentioned the robbery. Needless to say, Williams never saw the men again. One of them was described as 'five feet five, and rather lusty'.

1827: Thomas Smith and Alfred Cooper, described as 'well-known characters', were arrested for stealing Thomas Cox's silver watch during the fair. 'I felt a man's hand near my fob, and directly a tug, and found my watch gone', Cox reported. He confronted Smith and was threatened with violence, but the culprits were collared and sentenced to transportation for life – doing time, you might say.

1832: The following caution appeared this year:

The drunkard's coat of arms. (LC-USZ62-86047)

ST. GILES'S FAIR – CAUTION AND REMONSTRANCE – To all Drunkards and Revellers, and to the thoughtless and imprudent of both Sexes – You were told by the Oxford Board of Health on the 5th of last December, (about six months before the Indian disease [i.e. cholera] had reached this city), that those had been the greatest sufferers from cholera who had been in the habit of indulging most freely in spirituous liquors, and that the habits of life should be regular and temperate. You were told by the Board the same salutary truth on the 27th of last July, when the disease began to scatter death amongst us. You are now told for the third time, that death and drunkenness go hand in hand in these times of epidemic diseases... The Oxford Board of Health for

the third time admonishes and entreats you to forbear and to abstain from all acts of intemperance and imprudence. Beware of late and long sittings, dancings, revellings, surfeitings, and such like. Beware of mixed, crowded, and unknown companies in the distempered atmospheres of booths, show rooms, and canvas or boarded apartments... But especially beware of drunkenness, for it has been found to bite as a serpent and to sting as an adder. Many who have raised their cup in merriment to their lips, have in agony lamented their excesses, and at their deaths have left a last legacy of warning to the drunkard. Let all beware who think no cost too great for the purchase of present pleasure – Death smites with its surest and swiftest arrows the licentious and intemperate – the rash, fool-hardy, and imprudent.

1843: 'We regret to say that an occurrence of a serious nature took place on Tuesday afternoon. It seems that a horse ridden by a groom, and most imprudently brought into the fair, having been frightened by the noise, ran away through the crowd, and, in its progress, knocked down at least 20 persons, several of whom were severely hurt.'

1854: 'Enos Perth of Wantage, a travelling musician aged twenty-eight, died of cholera in Buckingham after allegedly contracting the disease at St. Giles's fair.'

1855: Alfred Taylor was 'charged with driving a horse and cart in a furious manner through St. Giles's fair on Monday afternoon, to the imminent danger of the public'. The Mayor himself had come close to being trampled underfoot. Taylor blamed his young and inexperienced horse, who had been startled by all the noise. This was a bad ploy: taking an inexperienced horse to the fair was added to the other charges and he was imprisoned for two weeks.

THE MURDER OF 'MATCHY'!

In November 1871, a woman was murdered near Binsey Lane. The victim was Betsy Richards, thirty-three, a prostitute and match-seller who usually went by the name of 'Matchy'. She was found with her head half severed from her body. Nothing had been stolen, and no motive was apparent. The case remains a mystery to this day.

1859: 'Mr. Bruton, proprietor of one of the theatres in the fair, was seriously injured in the eye by some mischievous person throwing a cracker at him; he was taken to the Infirmary, where his eye was attended to, but it is feared he will lose the sight of it. Several other persons were injured by this foolish practice of throwing crackers, which are not only dangerous from the nature of their composition in inflicting injury where they strike, but are also inflammable, for a young lady in the fair had her bonnet set on fire by one which struck it.'

1862: On 10 September a monkey 'from a show fresh from St Giles' Fair' decided that the show mustn't go on. It attacked its keeper at their next venue in Thame, biting him so badly on the face and body that he was hospitalised.

1863: 'A Kaffir, who ate rats in a raw state, attracted some curiosity – and disgust.'

1875: Homeless Joseph Kavanagh made the mistake of straying into St Giles' Fair early in the morning and 'was charged with wandering about the public streets, without any visible means of subsistence', a crime which saw him sentenced to twenty-one days' hard labour in prison.

1876-80: There had been a crackdown on the traditional 'weapons' of the fair, traditionally used by boisterous youths to accost passers-by. The offending arms were 'squirts, scratch-my-backs and crackers'. These items were now banned; but 'short India rubber whips' immediately took their place. In 1877 these were 'confiscated in great number', having inflicted more physical damage to their victims than the previously banned items. In 1878 the more innocuous sounding 'grass ticklers' took their place, gentle proof that there's always a new way to annoy people.

DEATH BY ELEPHANT

1872: George Cox died at Radcliffe Infirmary in Oxford, due to injuries received on the Wednesday after the fair. He had been on his way from Eynsham to Oxford to fetch some bricks when 'he met a caravan of wild beasts which had been to St Giles' Fair, and the horse he was driving took fright at an elephant'. Cox climbed down to calm his horse, but the elephant was too terrifying: the horse bolted, George was struck by the cart shaft and finished up under the wheels.

The elephant at St Giles' was less good-natured than this example: it caused a man's death.
(LC-USZ62-61675)

In 1879 the mayor ordered 'whips and other devices' to be banned and/or confiscated. But pranksters found 'a worse nuisance... the deliberate throwing of handfuls of flour, bran, rice and sawdust into the faces of promenaders'. In 1880 they added Cayenne pepper to their artilleries.

1880: A bad year. An overturned lamp at a toy stall led to a fire, which, in addition to burning down the stall, consumed the dress of a ten-year-old girl. She was extinguished before too much damage was done. The reporter also noted a 'larger supply of the rough element in the fair than usual', and a rash of pick-pockets. He was also sad to report the first fairground ride accident in Oxford's history, when a carriage on a steam roundabout broke and threw its occupants, a girl and a child, to the ground. They escaped with minor injuries.

1881: The train carrying St Giles' revellers back to Abingdon crashed in the station when its brakes failed. The engine was a write-off, and several people were injured.

1883: The first fairground death came this year when Frederick Burnard, 'coachman to the Rev. G.E. Woods of Trinity College' tried to light his pipe while riding the roundabout. He lost his balance, fell, and fractured his skull. The owner of the ride was cleared of any blame.

1887: 'There was a considerable amount of horse-play indulged in by a number

THE SHIPTON RAILWAY DISASTER

In December 1874, a 'terrible accident' occurred near Oxford. The coroner's jury had the distressing duty of viewing thirty-one mangled bodies: 'The train was crowded with passengers, for the most part journeying to various parts to spend Christmas with their friends. It was somewhat late at Oxford, and after starting was, no doubt, travelling at a fair rate of speed, when, on nearing Hampton Gay Church, where the line crosses an embankment... the tyre of one of the wheels of a carriage suddenly broke, and threw the vehicle off the rails... all rolled over the embankment in a state of ruin... In a moment after the crash the air was filled with the shrieks and screams of the wounded and dying... Altogether it was a scene of horror indescribable... At present there are thirty-one people lying dead at Oxford, and the injured and wounded are said to be upwards of seventy.'

of decently-dressed roughs, who cared neither for age nor sex in their mad career... One boy was injured at a swing, another had has face cut open with a piece of glass, several pieces of which were recklessly thrown about.'

1891: Thomas Goswell of Church St, St Ebbes, was sent to prison for seven days. 'The Mayor said such conduct as that of the prisoner brought disgrace upon the City; he turned a fair for amusement into a scene of disorder and riot by getting drunk, losing his senses and wanting to fight everybody.'

Electricity was the source of dubious fun this year too. Men wired themselves to primitive machines to 'measure the amount of electricity that could be borne... when small bets were made as to whose 'yelling point' would be highest, horrible grimaces and contortions being allowed, the 'yell' only to decide the contest.'

1892: A good year for injuries, notching up twelve, mainly through falls from rides. One of them was a fatality, when 'a young lady from Nuneham' attempted to save a child, with whom she had been riding, from slipping off his seat and injuring himself. In doing so she tumbled and fractured her skull. The boy bounced off her prostrate body to safety, so part of her ambition was posthumously fulfilled.

Another coach-related incident had caused a sensation in Oxford in the 1820s: George Allum, 'a stout-built young man,' was convicted on his own confession of robbing and desperately wounding William Piggott, driver of the Gloucester Wagon, on his way from Farrington. 'The prisoner burst out into laughter while the Judge was passing sentence!' reported the *Leicester Chronicle*.

In 1893 councillors, vicars and other moral do-gooders passed a motion to abolish the fair, and over the next few years the abolitionist movement gathered more steam than a wide Oxford street full of fairground rides. But, somehow, St Giles' slipped through their spoilsport fingers, and it survives to this day, complete with injuries, fights, dodgy burgers, and all the fun of the fair.

St Giles' Fair today.

MAY AND MAY NOT

Oxford's other most celebrated annual revelry is May Morning. Each 1 May crowds gather to hear choristers greet the dawn with a burst of song from the top of Magdalen College bell tower at the end of the High Street.

- The tower was completed in 1509, and when the choristers sang in that year it was to mark the death of Henry VII, a patron of the College, who had conveniently died that year.
- Henry's eldest son Arthur had visited the College (founded in 1465) a few times too: his premature death at the age of fifteen denied the world a flesh and blood King Arthur and gave us instead his younger brother, the debauched tyrant, serial wedlocker and church desecrator Henry VIII.
- The 'ancient' tradition (originating in the 1970s) of jumping off Magdalen Bridge into the River Cherwell after the May Morning ceremony has resulted in several injuries over the years. The river is only 2ft deep at this point, and the plummet guarantees bruises at the very least. In 1997 a participant was paralysed, and the bridge was closed for the next five years on 1 May. It was closed again after broken bones in 2005. The record for injuries in a single May Morning dive-in is forty – at an estimated cost to the Health Service of about £50,000, as a spoilsport councillor pointed out.
- Ironically the 'tradition' of bridge jumping was inspired by well-meaning officials such as this, after the council decided to ban the inebriated punting and skinny-dipping that had pre-dated it in the 1960s.

MINOR MISDEMEANOURS AT THE OED

SAMUEL JOHNSON MAY have given English its first dictionary, but it was James Augustus Henry Murray (1837-1915) who gave it the one that would stand forever as a monument to the language. He began work on the first Oxford English Dictionary (OED) in 1878, with an approach that is so familiar to us in this Wikipedia age, but quite revolutionary at the time – the soliciting of contributions. One man would not have enough hours in his lifetime to realize a work of this magnitude, but a few hundred like-minded lexicographers could see the job through – especially in a city that had the vast resources of the Bodleian Library in its midst.

Moving to Oxford in 1884, Murray built a 'scriptorium' in his garden on Banbury Road. Slips of paper with literary and other quotations arrived by the sackload, and even letters addressed with a minimalist 'Mr Murray, Oxford' found their way to him. The post generated by this backyard industry was such that the Post Office installed a bespoke post box (still standing) outside the house.

Amongst Murray's army of enthusiastic amateur researchers was one Dr W.C. Minor, a contributor with almost superhuman output, and academically faultless too. Minor was to contribute 12,000 quotations to the project; but during the nineteen years of compilation,

although written correspondence had been regular, Murray had never managed to meet Minor. This ice was about to be broken, he hoped, and in organising a celebratory Dictionary Dinner at Oxford in October 1897 one of the first people earmarked for an invite was the elusive doctor with the prodigious etymological know-how.

However, as reported in a *Strand* article of 1915, Minor replied to the invitation saying that he was too ill to attend the function. Instead, he invited Murray to visit him, giving the address of a mansion in Crowthorne, Berkshire. Determined to meet his man wherever and whenever, Murray took the train to Crowthorne, where he was met by a coachman and driven to a large country mansion on the edge of the town.

Ushered into a gloomy study, and taking appreciative note of its book-lined walls, Murray approached the very respectable looking middle-aged gentleman who was this private library's sole occupant. Murray gushed forth his appreciation, saying what a pleasure it was to meet at last his indispensable contributor Dr. W.C. Minor.

The owner of the mansion shook his hand, but announced that he was not Dr Minor. His name was Nicholson, and he was the Governor of Broadmoor Asylum for the Clinically Insane, just down the road in Crowthorne. Dr Minor, an American

Back of the Bodleian.

assumed, given the 'doctor' tag, that his man was a medical officer at the prison. Shocked, but keeping an admirably stiff upper lip, Murray noted of this revelation:

> I was of course deeply affected by the story, but as Dr. Minor had never in the least alluded to himself or his position, all I could do was to write to him more respectfully and kindly than before, so as to show no notice of this disclosure, which I feared might make some change in our relations.

The men met for the first time in 1891, and Murray visited, and wrote, constantly from then until his death, their conversations always centring on lexicographal matters. Which is just as well, given the other dominant themes in Minor's life.

William Chester Minor (1834-1920), a graduate of Yale Medical School, was plunged into the American Civil War as a surgeon serving in the Unionist Army. His experiences there, carrying out bloody army discipline (branding the letter 'D' on a deserter's face on one occasion) and witnessing the carnage of the battlefield (notably the Battle of the Wilderness of 1864 in which around 30,000 men died), unbalanced him. In the aftermath of the war he was posted in New York, where he seems to have spent much of his time, money and energies on New York prostitutes.

and former army surgeon, was his longest-serving inmate, committed here after being found guilty of murder.

Alas, the story is too good to be true. Murray did eventually meet Minor – several times in fact – and the man was indeed locked up at Broadmoor, but the meeting at the governor's house never took place. The writer of the *Strand* article in which the yarn first appeared was rebuked for his over-active imagination but the story was still widely believed, even after it had been refuted.

In reality, Murray appears to have become aware of his star contributor's unusual circumstances in 1889 when an American scholar made a chance remark about 'poor Dr Minor'. The facts tumbled forth and came as a great surprise to Murray, even though he had been sending correspondence to Minor for ten years using the address 'Broadmoor, Crowthorne, Berkshire'. He always

In 1868 he was committed to St Elizabeth's Hospital, a lunatic asylum in Washington, 'incapacitated by causes arising in the line of duty'; but by 1871 was deemed well enough to move to his own place in London. Sadly he chose the slums of Lambeth and revisited his predilection for seedy carnal delights. On 17 February 1872 Minor shot and killed George Merret, a man he had never seen before and who just happened to be in the wrong place at the wrong time. Minor was convinced that Merret was a burglar with evil intent, but it appears that the unfortunate soul was simply on his way to work, having a pregnant wife and six children to support.

Rebranded as 'Patient 747', the doctor was sentenced to Broadmoor Asylum for the Criminally Insane, with the recommendation that he should never be released. It wasn't just the murder: Minor had violent visions and impulses of rage, and sexual fantasies clouded his thoughts. He was also inclined to self-mutilation during his darkest moments.

But, confined and medicated, the fact that he was an educated and wealthy man brought certain privileges, namely twin, private rooms in the prison, an ever-growing book collection, and materials for

Churchill, who engineered the move of Minor to the USA.

painting pictures (a hobby he shared with fellow inmate, the famously insane painter Richard Dadd, committed here after cutting his father's throat with a razor).

It was his large stash of sixteenth- and seventeenth-century volumes that provided the meat for Minor's major research. Since finding Murray's original leaflet asking for contributions in 1880 ('An Appeal to the English-speaking and English-reading Public', which some far-fetched versions of the story say was brought into the prison by George Merret's widow Eliza), he had focused his attentions on words. He sometimes delivered over a hundred etymological glosses a week (i.e. examples of word usage – this is the chief aim of the OED, which does not just define all English words but illustrates its definitions by quoting original, written contexts). Murray once declared of Minor's contributions 'that we could easily illustrate the last four centuries from his quotations alone'.

In 1902 Minor reminded everyone how disturbed he really was, in spite of all the academia, by cutting off his penis. Distressed admirers such as Murray now began to campaign for his return to America, where the doctor wished to end his days.

The change of scenery was finally sanctioned in 1910. Murray and his wife Ada came to wave off the seventy-six-year-old prisoner, who was transferred back to St Elizabeth Hospital in Washington – a switch engineered in part by no lesser a sympathiser than the Home Secretary, a certain Winston Churchill. This unique bedrock of the OED died in 1920, while Murray passed away five years earlier at his Oxford home.

OXFORD IN SHOCK

The War Years

OXFORD MANAGED TO avoid the Zeppelin raids of the First World War, and would enjoy similar good fortune when the Luftwaffe droned over much of the island twenty-five years later. But the city still had its share of the general misery of the two wars.

In May 1917, when forty-eight-year-old American surgeon Harvey Cushing, attached to the British Expeditionary Force in France, arrived in Oxford on a flying visit, the casualties of war were in full view. The Thames was choked with boats carrying convalescent soldiers; the Examination Schools had given way to a very different form of examination, filled with makeshift hospital beds overflowing with wounded men; and in the grounds of New College there was a shanty town of hospital tents, housing soldiers suffering from shell-shock. These tents were huddled beneath the ancient town wall that had survived the centuries in the College grounds.

Psychological disorder was the specialist area of Oxford academic William McDougall, who held the University post of Wilde Reader in Mental Philosophy between 1904 and 1920. Over lunch at his house in Littlemore, soon after Cushing's arrival, McDougall described to his guest the new phenomenon of 'shell shock', for which several men had already been unfairly executed on the front line, the severe mental illness crudely interpreted as cowardice and desertion. To illustrate the condition vividly, he outlined to Cushing the case of one of the New College shanty-town residents, not troubling posterity with the man's name, merely saying that the patient was a soldier in the regular army.

The soldier had been on the front line for two years, surviving such iconic arenas of war as Mons and the Somme. He was said to have gone 'over the top' in battle nineteen times. Two months previous to Cushing's visit the soldier had been caught in a British 'friendly fire' artillery barrage, and had seen most of his comrades die. After this tragedy he had fought his way to a shelled German dugout and taken prisoners. A British officer then arrived – but instead of commending the man he brushed him aside and shot all the prisoners with his revolver. This sent the soldier over the edge, and he showed the first symptoms of shell shock – uncontrollable trembling, involuntary twitching, a heightened state of panic, and the tendency to weep.

McDougall explained to Cushing that men such as his unfortunate subject were suffering a mental disorder. The condition had first been noted just two years previously as 'an orgy of neuroses and psychoses and gaits and paralyses', and was thought to be the result of an invasion of the central nervous system or the brain – either by toxic gases or tiny fragments

STRAY NOTES FROM WORLD WAR ONE

- The lack of Zeppelin attacks on Oxford was attributed by writer Joseph Wells to silence: 'During the war Tom [i.e. the bell at Christ Church College] was forbidden to sound, along with all the other Oxford bells and clocks, for might not his mighty voice have guided some Zeppelin or German aeroplane to pour down destruction on Oxford? Few things brought home more to Oxford the meaning of the Armistice than hearing Tom once more on the night of November 11, 1918.' (*The Charm of Oxford*, 1920.)
- The Wilfred Owen Archive is kept by Oxford University. Owen was killed just a week before the Armistice, having taken the decision to remain at the front to chronicle the war, taking the place of fellow poet, friend and mentor Siegfried Sassoon (one-time Oxford resident) who had been wounded in the head during an unfortunate incident of 'friendly fire'. Sassoon was horrified, threatening to stab Owen in order to invalid him out of the army.
- Other 'War Poets' with connection to the city include Lincoln College alumnus Edward Thomas, whose eulogy to the city, *Oxford*, was published in 1903. Like Owen, he died during the conflict.
- Writer Vera Brittain, of Somerville College, lost most of her loved ones in the First World War, including her fiancé and brother. She became a nursing auxiliary, studied in Oxford again after the war, and became a successful writer and speaker. Her fame as a 'principled pacifist' and her influential voice on the international stage is underlined poignantly by her inclusion in Hitler's notorious 'Black Book', which named 2,000 people to be immediately arrested in Britain after the Germans invaded.
- Oxford enjoyed more peacetime in the First World War than Britain at large: due to inefficient communications, news of the declaration of war took more than two days to reach Oxford Town Hall.
- Prime Minister-to-be Harold Macmillan was wounded three times in the war, and never returned to complete his degree at Balliol. He commented later: 'I could not face it. It was a city of ghosts'.
- 2,700 University men were killed in the 1914-18 war – 18 per cent of 15,000 or so members who enlisted. Corpus Christi College lost 25 per cent of its members, and New College lost the most individuals – 257.

The eyes of the soldier in the sling tell it all: a typical case of shell shock at the Front.

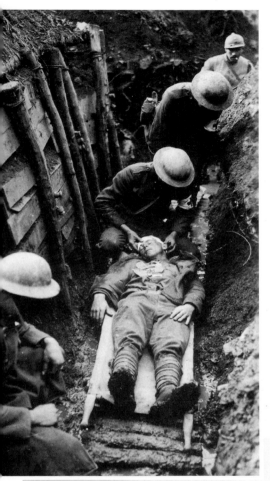

The disturbing sights that British men were forced to confront during the war caused enormous psychological damage; suffering men flooded into Oxford. (NARA, 530724)

The terrible effects of poison gas at the Front: it damaged soldiers for years after the conflict had ended. (NARA, 530749)

of explosives. McDougall had been one of the observers to realise that the syndrome was a psychological disorder brought on by exposure to trench warfare and the horrors it inflicted on all the human senses.

McDougall had chosen this particular victim as an illustration due to an unfortunate incident the night before. The man had been 'making good progress', according to the doctor, but in the night a section of that ancient town wall in New College had collapsed around the convalescent's tent, and his symptoms had returned in force.

The eminent psychologist's interest in his subjects was purely academic, though. Renowned as arrogant and aloof, McDougall advocated 'positive eugenics' of the sort espoused by many proto-fascists in the pre-Holocaust era, horrified at the huge families raised by the average working-class man. The aim of these eugenics was to filter out low intellect, and McDougall proposed improving the bright spark/two short planks ratio by offering University dons, civil servants and other members of the intelligentsia financial incentives for raising big families. Failing to lead from the front, however, he only managed five children himself.

McDougall moaned to Cushing about his frustrating lack of University facilities. There was nowhere to carry out experimental work, he claimed – and given his attitude to the 'surplus population' it's just as well. Oxford had not yet accepted the validity of Psychology as a discipline separate from Philosophy, and the University's Philosophers belittled the upstarts who were attempting to steal a chapter of their chosen subject.

Given this uphill struggle, McDougall confessed that the war 'was a wonderful experience for a psychologist', with a 'most strange, wonderful and pitiful collection of nervously disordered soldiers'. In spite of his personal disdain for the common man,

in the field of his research he said that 'sympathetic rapport' with the victim was the key to understanding.

As Cushing listened with mounting alarm, McDougall described men whose shell-shock symptoms returned when they tried to shave; when they were in railway carriages; or when they saw soldiers in uniform. He spoke of a man who had screamed during a mortar attack at Gallipoli and had not managed to close his mouth several months later; of an amnesiac who had handily forgotten that he was about to leave his unfaithful wife; and a small number of victims who had retreated so far into themselves that they behaved like helpless babies.

Cushing returned to his work tending American servicemen on the battlefront, thinking himself lucky that his own brief was to sort out physical rather than psychological mishap, and convinced that his own skills as a brain surgeon had little bearing on the phenomenon of shell shock.

McDougall opened an outpatient clinic for shell-shock sufferers at the Radcliffe Infirmary in 1918, and left Oxford for Harvard in 1920. He was replaced in the Wilde chair by William Brown, described by poet (and imminent war casualty) Wilfred Owen as 'a regular magician, who mesmerises when he pleases'. By this time psychology was being taken seriously as a subject in academic Oxford, but Brown had inherited some of his predecessor's predilection for controversy. In 1937 he publicly declared that Hitler was 'the greatest psychotherapist of the nations'. When trying to squirm out of this statement in 1940, Brown insisted that his aim in making the statement had been to gain a personal audience with Hitler, and to use his skills in hypnosis to 'divert him from his mad course of destruction'.

On an equally cheeky note, Brown is said to have procured money for a second

Readership in Psychology after persuading a rich benefactress, under hypnosis, to offer an endowment.

ENGLAND'S LAST WOLF HUNT

On 26 January 1937, just a few years before the outbreak of the Second World War, Oxford Zoo's three wolves escaped. Somehow the door had been left open after feeding time, and the animals bolted, clearing a way through the sparsely populated zoo precincts and exiting through the main gates into suburban Kidlington. Panic reigned, and police marksmen were called in to gun down the lupine fugitives.

If they made it into the woodlands of the surrounding countryside, the wolves were in with a decent chance of evading the guns, at least for a few days. The terrain was not familiar to them however, and one – an impressive male measuring nearly 2 metres – loped down the Banbury Road towards Oxford instead, causing uproar amongst the indigenous dog population. Inspector Barnett of the City Police did the honours, shooting the beast dead as it neared the police houses that stood on that thoroughfare, just a couple of hours after the escape.

The survivors kept to the open countryside, but by now the entire county was on red alert. Robert Collett of Hampton Poyle spotted something big and bad huffing and puffing around his father's farm, and bagged wolf number two on that same evening. But by nightfall the third wolf had evaded capture.

From a reporter's point of view, this was a very welcome outcome. It gave the local and national newspapers the opportunity to report the incident, and to give readers a 'To be continued...' true-life-drama story that few can resist.

Grilled about the incident, Zoo Director Captain W.F. Cooper – of Cooper's Oxford Marmalade fame – reassured the public. The surviving wolf, he said, was a hand-reared female, just fourteen months old and very timid. So confident was he that she would not stray too far from her home that he had left the zoo gates open, placing a tempting hunk of meat in a makeshift kennel close to the entrance, summoning the wolf to supper. She would, Cooper asserted, be very hungry after her ordeal, being quite incapable of killing anything for herself. It was almost as if he were blaming the other two wolves for the breakout, the poor fourteen-month female a mere dupe in their criminal enterprise.

Two keepers stayed up all night waiting for the wolf's return, but she failed to appear. In the small hours a trigger-happy hunter gunned down something wolfish in a rickyard at nearby Thrupp, revealing afterwards that he had pursued the beast for 2 miles overground. Embarrassingly, the carcass turned out to be someone's pet German Shepherd.

Tracks, meanwhile, were found at Islip, north-east of the city, after the wolf was spotted by the driver of a passing train. She was also glimpsed flitting ghost-like through car headlights in Islip. Four dead chickens were brought forth as evidence of her blood-thirstiness, but closer examination proved this to be the work of a fox. A local party of hunters then took up the scent and chased the wolf along the River Ray towards the wilderness of Otmoor: as suitable a haunt for a wolf as any in the south of England.

The huntsmen lost their prey in the gathering gloom, but on the following day the wolf was seen once again in Islip. This time she was clearly very tired and nervous, running from farm to farm in an apparent bid to find the kind of shelter – i.e. man-made – to which she was accustomed.

On the 28th a photographer from the *Oxford Mail*, Johnny Johnson, teamed up with Captain Cooper's son Dennis, packing sandwiches in preparation for a long day's wolf hunting. Reports had suggested that the animal was heading south west, back towards the zoo. She had wandered too far from home to pick up the scent of the hunk of meat in the purpose-built kennel, and had taken drastic action to secure some sustenance, killing not just one but thirteen sheep on a farm near North Oxford Golf Club, all reportedly 'bitten through the throat'. A leg from one of the

BEASTLY OXFORD

- Oxford Zoo was open between 1931 and 1937. Its star turns included Rosie the Elephant, Hanno the Lion, and a 'winged cat' captured locally in 1934, and said to use its dragon-like appendages to assist in jumping. After closure, W. Frank 'Marmalade' Cooper moved the zoo stock to a new establishment at Dudley – with the exception of Rosie, who went to Bristol. The zoo site is now the HQ of Thames Valley Police.

- Wolves had often visited Oxford in the past as part of the travelling menageries associated with St Giles' Fair in September each year. The show in 1893 included a booth containing one Captain Rowland, armed with a hot iron bar for safety, in a cage with wolves, a 'Russian bear' and two lionesses. This was the event's biggest attraction, but not everyone enjoyed it: fearful audience members shouted to be let out, but were unable to get through the huge crowd to the exit. As the reporter in *Jackson's Oxford Journal* put it: 'whether they wished it or not they were obliged to have their money's worth'.

- This history of Oxford starts and ends in lupine fashion. Wolves, you may recall, feature in the legendary origins of Oxford. According to folklore the city was founded by King Memphric in 1009 BC. Evil to the core, Memphric was hated by his subjects, and everyone breathed a sigh of relief when, during a hunting trip, he was cornered by wolves and devoured. The location of this fatal encounter was afterwards called Wolvercote – just a stone's throw from where Johnson bagged Oxford's last wolf.

Another animal caused a sensation at Wolvercote in 1830: a duck. One Mr Thomas Beesley stole it, stuffing it into his pocket. However, the duck quacked and gave him away. A passer-by tried to wrestle the duck from him, and in the fight that ensued sixteen-year-old John Barrett was struck on the head with a truncheon and killed. Beesley was found guilty of manslaughter and sentenced to fourteen years' transportation.

STRAY NOTES FROM WORLD WAR TWO

- The Morris car factory at Cowley produced 650 tanks during the war, while William Morris' sister business, the Pressed Steel Company, normally pressing steel car bodies, churned out thousands of cartridge cases, employing a largely female workforce.
- Members of the University and Oxford University Press were employed to write and produce pro-Allied forces propaganda leaflets in German.
- Hitler's decision not to bomb Oxford was said to be based on the city's central location and his admiration of its architecture. It was to be his main base in England following German victory in the war.
- Edward F. Halifax, viceroy to India and ambassador to the US, stated soon after the Second World War: 'I often think how much easier the world would have been to manage if Herr Hitler and Signor Mussolini had been at Oxford.'
- The Oxford University Air Squadron (OUAS) was the source of many fighters in the Battle of Britain, including Spitfire ace Richard Hillary, shot down twice in 1939 after taking down several enemy planes. Rising again from extensive plastic surgery – an area pioneered at Oxford – he was shot down for the last time in 1943.
- The most famous member of the OUAS was Group Captain Leonard Cheshire. Awarded the Victoria Cross, it was after his 103rd mission as official British observer of the nuclear bombing of Nagasaki that his life changed. From then on he poured his money and efforts into charitable works, the most lasting being the health and welfare charity the Leonard Cheshire Foundation (called Leonard Cheshire Disability since 2007).
- Penicillin was developed in Oxford during the war as the world's first antibiotic. First described by Alexander Fleming in 1925, it was Nazi Germany refugee Ernst Chain and Rhodes Scholar Howard Florey who developed it as a drug fit for mass production. Their guinea pig was an Oxford policeman who was dying from an infected wound inflicted while pruning roses. The drug worked near-miracles, but supplies ran out. Traces were recycled from the policeman's urine, but not enough to save his life.

Lord Edward F. Halifax (centre, in hat) at Roosevelt's inauguration. (LC-USW3-057072-C)

flock was found a kilometre away from the field of carnage. No fox was going to take the blame for this little lot.

At which point the sanguine Zoo Director probably realised that his beloved fourteen-month-old she-wolf was not going to have a happy ending. Inspector Barnett, killer of the Banbury Road beast, had seen her 'hanging on to the throat of another sheep' (according to a report in *The Times*). He and the flock's owner had run at the wolf, and she had let them cover a 100 metres before beating a sheepish retreat.

This time the wolf, enlivened by a good feed, hurtled down into Oxford, probably searching for zoo and home.

Instead she met Johnson and Cooper, the former putting aside his camera and reaching for his gun as she bounded into view in Summertown. Spotting her would-be assassins, the wolf fled, but had the misfortune to run into a gaggle of screaming children. Turning back in fear, she headed towards the A40 bypass.

According to his own report, intrepid Johnson commandeered a bike from a cyclist and kept up with the beast's progress by following the sound of people shouting: 'There's the wolf, there's the wolf!' From 30 yards he took the best shot of his career, killing her with a single round. It wasn't exactly good publicity for the zoo, though, which closed that same year.

BIBLIOGRAPHY

Anonymous, *History, Gazetteer and Directory of the County of Oxford* (Peterborough, 1852)

Clark, Sir George, *Oxford and the Civil War* (pamphlet, Oxford, 1970)

Cox, George Valentine, *Recollections of Oxford* (London, 1868)

Craik, George Lillie, *The Pictorial History of England: being a history of the people as well as a history of the Kingdom* (London, 1838)

Davenport, John Marriott, *Oxfordshire Annals* (Oxford, 1869)

Davies, Norman, *The Isles* (London, 1999)

Ditchfield, P.H. (editor) *Memorials of Old Oxfordshire* (London 1903)

Foxe, John, *The Book of Martyrs* (Foxe's Book of Martyrs) (London 1563)

Goldwyn Smith, D.C.L., *Oxford and her Colleges* (London, 1895)

Ingram, James, *Memorials of Oxford* (Oxford, 1837)

Jeaffreson, John Cordy, *Annals of Oxford* (London, 1871)

Knapp, Andrew and Baldwin, William, *The Newgate Calendar* (London 1824)

Lang, Andrew, *Oxford: Brief Historical and Descriptive Notes* (Oxford, 1880)

Morris, Jan, *Oxford* (Oxford, 1978)

Morris, Jan, *The Oxford Book of Oxford* (Oxford, 1978)

Murray, John (editor), *A Handbook for Travellers in Berks, Bucks, and Oxfordshire: Including a Particular Description of the University and City of Oxford and the Descent of the Thames to Maidenhead and Windsor* (London, 1860).

Parker, James, *The Early History of Oxford, 727-1100, preceded by a sketch of the mythical origin of the city and University* (London, 1885)

Rapin, Paul de, *The History of England, Volume I*, translated by Nicolas Tindal (London 1732)

Roberson, George and Green, John Richard, *Oxford During the Last Century: being two series of papers published in the* Oxford Chronicle & Berks & Bucks Gazette *During the Year 1859* (Oxford, 1859)

Spiers, R.A.H., *Round About 'The Mitre' at Oxford* (Oxford 1929)

Sullivan, Paul, *Oxford: A Pocket Miscellany* (Stroud, 2011)

Sullivan, Paul, *A Little Book of Oxfordshire* (Stroud, 2012)

Tames, Richard, *A Traveller's History of Oxford* (London, 2002)

Walker, Rev John, *Oxoniana: or anecdotes relative to the University and city of Oxford*, Volume 1 (Oxford, 1806)

Wells, Joseph, *The Charm of Oxford* (London 1921)

Whittock, Nathaniel, *Topographical and Historical Description of the University and City of Oxford* (London, 1828)

Wood, Anthony and Hearne, Thomas, *The Life of Anthony à Wood from the Year 1632 to 1672* (Oxford, 1772)

Wood, Anthony and Peshall, John, *The Antient and Present State of the City of Oxford* (London, 1773)

NEWSPAPERS AND MAGAZINES

Jackson's Oxford Journal, 1753-1928
The Times
The Daily Telegraph
The Oxford Mail
The Oxford Times
Oxford Today, the University Magazine
Oxfordshire Limited Edition
Other regional newspaper archives

WEBSITES

University and Colleges portal: www.ox.ac.uk/colleges
Wikipedia: en.wikipedia.org
www.headington.org.uk
www.oxfordcityguide.com
www.inoxfordmag.co.uk
www.berkshirehistory.com
www.dailyinfo.co.uk
www.oxford.gov.uk
www.british-history.ac.uk
www.shotover.clara.net